INTERNATIONAL FINANCIAL STATEMENT ANALYSIS WORKBOOK

CFA Institute is the premier association for investment professionals around the world, with over 124,000 members in 145 countries. Since 1963 the organization has developed and administered the renowned Chartered Financial Analyst® Program. With a rich history of leading the investment profession, CFA Institute has set the highest standards in ethics, education, and professional excellence within the global investment community and is the foremost authority on investment profession conduct and practice.

Each book in the CFA Institute Investment Series is geared toward industry practitioners along with graduate-level finance students and covers the most important topics in the industry. The authors of these cutting-edge books are themselves industry professionals and academics and bring their wealth of knowledge and expertise to this series.

INTERNATIONAL FINANCIAL STATEMENT ANALYSIS WORKBOOK

Third Edition

Thomas R. Robinson, CFA

Elaine Henry, CFA

Wendy L. Pirie, CFA

Michael A. Broihahn, CFA

WILEY

ISBN 978-1-118-99948-6 (Hardcover)
ISBN 978-1-119-02971-7 (ePDF)
ISBN 978-1-119-02972-4 (ePub)

Printed in the United States of America.
10 9 8

CONTENTS

INTERNATIONAL FINANCIAL STATEMENT ANALYSIS WORKBOOK

PART I

LEARNING OUTCOMES, SUMMARY OVERVIEW, AND PROBLEMS

CHAPTER 1

FINANCIAL STATEMENT ANALYSIS: AN INTRODUCTION

LEARNING OUTCOMES

After completing this chapter, you will be able to do the following:

- describe the roles of financial reporting and financial statement analysis;
- describe the roles of the key financial statements (statement of financial position, statement of comprehensive income, statement of changes in equity, and statement of cash flows) in evaluating a company's performance and financial position;
- describe the importance of financial statement notes and supplementary information—including disclosures of accounting policies, methods, and estimates—and management's commentary;
- describe the objective of audits of financial statements, the types of audit reports, and the importance of effective internal controls;
- identify and describe information sources that analysts use in financial statement analysis besides annual financial statements and supplementary information;
- describe the steps in the financial statement analysis framework.

SUMMARY OVERVIEW

- The primary purpose of financial reports is to provide information and data about a company's financial position and performance, including profitability and cash flows. The information presented in financial reports—including the financial statements and notes—and other reports—including management's commentary or management's discussion and analysis—allows the financial analyst to assess a company's financial position and performance and trends in that performance.
- The basic financial statements are the statement of financial position (i.e., the balance sheet), the statement of comprehensive income (i.e., a single statement of comprehensive income

or two statements consisting of an income statement and a statement of comprehensive income), the statement of changes in equity, and the statement of cash flows.

- The balance sheet discloses what resources a company controls (assets) and what it owes (liabilities) at a specific point in time. Owners' equity represents the net assets of the company; it is the owners' residual interest in or residual claim on the company's assets after deducting its liabilities. The relationship among the three parts of the balance sheet (assets, liabilities, and owners' equity) may be shown in equation form as follows: Assets = Liabilities + Owners' equity.

- The income statement presents information on the financial results of a company's business activities over a period of time. The income statement communicates how much revenue and other income the company generated during a period and what expenses, including losses, it incurred in connection with generating that revenue and other income. The basic equation underlying the income statement is Revenue + Other income − Expenses = Net income.

- The statement of comprehensive income includes all items that change owners' equity except transactions with owners. Some of these items are included as part of net income, and some are reported as other comprehensive income (OCI).

- The statement of changes in equity provides information about increases or decreases in the various components of owners' equity.

- Although the income statement and balance sheet provide measures of a company's success, cash and cash flow are also vital to a company's long-term success. Disclosing the sources and uses of cash helps creditors, investors, and other statement users evaluate the company's liquidity, solvency, and financial flexibility.

- The notes (also referred to as footnotes) that accompany the financial statements are an integral part of those statements and provide information that is essential to understanding the statements. Analysts should evaluate note disclosures regarding the use of alternative accounting methods, estimates, and assumptions.

- In addition to the financial statements, a company provides other sources of information that are useful to the financial analyst. As part of his or her analysis, the financial analyst should read and assess this additional information, particularly that presented in the management commentary (also called management report[ing], operating and financial review, and management's discussion and analysis [MD&A]).

- A publicly traded company must have an independent audit performed on its annual financial statements. The auditor's report expresses an opinion on the financial statements and provides some assurance about whether the financial statements fairly present a company's financial position, performance, and cash flows. In addition, for US publicly traded companies, auditors must also express an opinion on the company's internal control systems.

- Information on the economy, industry, and peer companies is useful in putting the company's financial performance and position in perspective and in assessing the company's future. In most cases, information from sources apart from the company are crucial to an analyst's effectiveness.

- The financial statement analysis framework provides steps that can be followed in any financial statement analysis project. These steps are:
  - articulate the purpose and context of the analysis;
  - collect input data;
  - process data;
  - analyze/interpret the processed data;
  - develop and communicate conclusions and recommendations; and
  - follow up.

PROBLEMS

1. Providing information about the performance and financial position of companies so that users can make economic decisions *best* describes the role of:
   A. auditing.
   ✓ B. financial reporting.
   ‣ C. financial statement analysis.

2. A company's current financial position would *best* be evaluated using the:
   ⟩ A. balance sheet.
   B. income statement.
   C. statement of cash flows.

3. A company's profitability for a period would *best* be evaluated using the:
   A. balance sheet.
   ✓ B. income statement.
   C. statement of cash flows.

4. Accounting policies, methods, and estimates used in preparing financial statements are *most likely* found in the:
   A. auditor's report.
   B. management commentary.
   ✓ C. notes to the financial statements.

5. Information about management and director compensation would *least likely* be found in the:
   ✓ A. auditor's report.
   B. proxy statement.
   C. notes to the financial statements.

6. Information about a company's objectives, strategies, and significant risks would *most likely* be found in the:
   A. auditor's report.
   ✓ B. management commentary.
   C. notes to the financial statements.

7. What type of audit opinion is preferred when analyzing financial statements?
   A. Qualified.
   B. Adverse.
   ✓ C. Unqualified.

8. Ratios are an input into which step in the financial statement analysis framework?
   A. Process data.
   B. Collect input data.
   ✓ C. Analyze/interpret the processed data.

CHAPTER 2

FINANCIAL REPORTING MECHANICS

LEARNING OUTCOMES

After completing this chapter, you will be able to do the following:

- explain the relationship of financial statement elements and accounts, and classify accounts into the financial statement elements;
- explain the accounting equation in its basic and expanded forms;
- describe the process of recording business transactions using an accounting system based on the accounting equation;
- describe the need for accruals and other adjustments in preparing financial statements;
- describe the relationships among the income statement, balance sheet, statement of cash flows, and statement of owners' equity;
- describe the flow of information in an accounting system;
- describe the use of the results of the accounting process in security analysis.

SUMMARY OVERVIEW

- Business activities can be classified into three groups: operating activities, investing activities, and financing activities.
- Companies classify transactions into common accounts that are components of the five financial statement elements: assets, liabilities, equity, revenue, and expense.

- The core of the accounting process is the basic accounting equation: Assets = Liabilities + Owners' equity.
- The expanded accounting equation is Assets = Liabilities + Contributed capital + Beginning retained earnings + Revenue − Expenses − Dividends.
- Business transactions are recorded in an accounting system that is based on the basic and expanded accounting equations.
- The accounting system tracks and summarizes data used to create financial statements: the balance sheet, income statement, statement of cash flows, and statement of owners' equity. The statement of retained earnings is a component of the statement of owners' equity.
- Accruals are a necessary part of the accounting process and are designed to allocate activity to the proper period for financial reporting purposes.
- The results of the accounting process are financial reports that are used by managers, investors, creditors, analysts, and others in making business decisions.
- An analyst uses the financial statements to make judgments on the financial health of a company.
- Company management can manipulate financial statements, and a perceptive analyst can use his or her understanding of financial statements to detect misrepresentations.

PROBLEMS

1. Which of the following items would most likely be classified as an operating activity?
   A. Issuance of debt.
   B. Acquisition of a competitor.
   C. Sale of automobiles by an automobile dealer.

2. Which of the following items would most likely be classified as a financing activity?
   A. Issuance of debt.
   B. Payment of income taxes.
   C. Investments in the stock of a supplier.

3. Which of the following elements represents an economic resource?
   A. Asset.
   B. Liability.
   C. Owners' equity.

4. Which of the following elements represents a residual claim?
   A. Asset.
   B. Liability.
   C. Owners' equity.

5. An analyst has projected that a company will have assets of €2,000 at year-end and liabilities of €1,200. The analyst's projection of total owners' equity should be *closest* to:
   A. €800.
   B. €2,000.
   C. €3,200.

6. An analyst has collected the following information regarding a company in advance of its year-end earnings announcement (in millions):

Estimated net income	$	200
Beginning retained earnings	$	1,400
Estimated distributions to owners	$	100

The analyst's estimate of ending retained earnings (in millions) should be *closest* to:
   A. $1,300.
   B. $1,500.
   C. $1,700.

7. An analyst has compiled the following information regarding Rubsam, Inc.

Liabilities at year-end	€	1,000
Contributed capital at year-end	€	500
Beginning retained earnings	€	600
Revenue during the year	€	5,000
Expenses during the year	€	4,300

There have been no distributions to owners. The analyst's *most likely* estimate of total assets at year-end should be *closest* to:
   A. €2,100.
   B. €2,300.
   C. €2,800.

8. A group of individuals formed a new company with an investment of $500,000. The *most likely* effect of this transaction on the company's accounting equation at the time of the formation is an increase in cash and:
   A. an increase in revenue.
   B. an increase in liabilities.
   C. an increase in contributed capital.

9. HVG, LLC paid $12,000 of cash to a real estate company upon signing a lease on 31 December 2005. The payment represents a $4,000 security deposit and $4,000 of rent for each of January 2006 and February 2006. Assuming that the correct accounting is to reflect both January and February rent as prepaid, the *most likely* effect on HVG's accounting equation in December 2005 is:
   A. no net change in assets.
   B. a decrease in assets of $8,000.
   C. a decrease in assets of $12,000.

10. TRR Enterprises sold products to customers on 30 June 2006 for a total price of €10,000. The terms of the sale are that payment is due in 30 days. The cost of the products was €8,000. The *most likely* net change in TRR's total assets on 30 June 2006 related to this transaction is:
   A. €0.
   B. €2,000.
   C. €10,000.

11. On 30 April 2006, Pinto Products received a cash payment of $30,000 as a deposit on production of a custom machine to be delivered in August 2006. This transaction would *most likely* result in which of the following on 30 April 2006?
   A. No effect on liabilities.
   B. A decrease in assets of $30,000.
   C. An increase in liabilities of $30,000.

12. Squires & Johnson, Ltd., recorded €250,000 of depreciation expense in December 2005. The *most likely* effect on the company's accounting equation is:
   A. no effect on assets.
   B. a decrease in assets of €250,000.
   C. an increase in liabilities of €250,000.

13. An analyst who is interested in assessing a company's financial position is *most likely* to focus on which financial statement?
   A. Balance sheet.
   B. Income statement.
   C. Statement of cash flows.

14. The statement of cash flows presents the flows into which three groups of business activities?
   A. Operating, Nonoperating, and Financing.
   B. Operating, Investing, and Financing.
   C. Operating, Nonoperating, and Investing.

15. Which of the following statements about cash received prior to the recognition of revenue in the financial statements is *most* accurate? The cash is recorded as:
   A. deferred revenue, an asset.
   B. accrued revenue, a liability.
   C. deferred revenue, a liability.

16. When, at the end of an accounting period, a revenue has been recognized in the financial statements but no billing has occurred and no cash has been received, the accrual is to:
   A. unbilled (accrued) revenue, an asset.
   B. deferred revenue, an asset.
   C. unbilled (accrued) revenue, a liability.

17. When, at the end of an accounting period, cash has been paid with respect to an expense, the business should then record:
   A. an accrued expense, an asset.
   B. a prepaid expense, an asset.
   C. an accrued expense, a liability.

18. When, at the end of an accounting period, cash has not been paid with respect to an expense that has been incurred, the business should then record:
   A. an accrued expense, an asset.
   B. a prepaid expense, an asset.
   C. an accrued expense, a liability.

19. The collection of all business transactions sorted by account in an accounting system is referred to as:
    A. a trial balance.
    B. a general ledger.
    C. a general journal.

20. If a company reported fictitious revenue, it could try to cover up its fraud by:
    A. decreasing assets.
    B. increasing liabilities.
    C. creating a fictitious asset.

CHAPTER 3

FINANCIAL
REPORTING STANDARDS

LEARNING OUTCOMES

After completing this chapter, you will be able to do the following:

- describe the objective of financial statements and the importance of financial reporting standards in security analysis and valuation;
- describe roles and desirable attributes of financial reporting standard-setting bodies and regulatory authorities in establishing and enforcing reporting standards, and describe the role of the International Organization of Securities Commissions;
- describe the status of global convergence of accounting standards and ongoing barriers to developing one universally accepted set of financial reporting standards;
- describe the International Accounting Standards Board's conceptual framework, including the objective and qualitative characteristics of financial statements, required reporting elements, and constraints and assumptions in preparing financial statements;
- describe general requirements for financial statements under International Financial Reporting Standards (IFRS);
- compare key concepts of financial reporting standards under IFRS and US generally accepted accounting principles (US GAAP) reporting systems;
- identify characteristics of a coherent financial reporting framework and the barriers to creating such a framework;
- describe implications for financial analysis of differing financial reporting systems and the importance of monitoring developments in financial reporting standards;
- analyze company disclosures of significant accounting policies.

SUMMARY OVERVIEW

- *The Objective of Financial Reporting*:
  - The objective of general purpose financial reporting is to provide financial information about the reporting entity that is useful to existing and potential investors, lenders, and other creditors in making decisions about providing resources to the entity. Those decisions involve buying, selling, or holding equity and debt instruments, and providing or settling loans and other forms of credit.[1]
  - Financial reporting requires policy choices and estimates. These choices and estimates require judgment, which can vary from one preparer to the next. Accordingly, standards are needed to ensure increased consistency in these judgments.
- *Financial Reporting Standard-Setting Bodies and Regulatory Authorities*: Private sector standard-setting bodies and regulatory authorities play significant but different roles in the standard-setting process. In general, standard-setting bodies make the rules, and regulatory authorities enforce the rules. However, regulators typically retain legal authority to establish financial reporting standards in their jurisdiction.
- *Convergence of Global Financial Reporting Standards*: The IASB and FASB, along with other standard setters, are working to achieve convergence of financial reporting standards. Many countries have adopted or permit the use of IFRS, have indicated that they will adopt IFRS in the future, or have indicated that they are working on convergence with IFRS. Listed companies in many countries are adopting IFRS. Barriers and challenges to full convergence still exist.
- *The IFRS Framework*: The IFRS *Framework* sets forth the concepts that underlie the preparation and presentation of financial statements for external users, provides further guidance on the elements from which financial statements are constructed, and discusses concepts of capital and capital maintenance.
  - The objective of fair presentation of useful information is the center of the *Conceptual Framework (2010)*. The qualitative characteristics of useful information include fundamental and enhancing characteristics. Information must exhibit the fundamental characteristics of relevance and faithful representation to be useful. The enhancing characteristics identified are comparability, verifiability, timeliness, and understandability.
  - The IFRS *Framework* identifies the following elements of financial statements: assets, liabilities, equity, income, expenses, and capital maintenance adjustments.
  - The *Conceptual Framework (2010)* is constructed based on the underlying assumptions of accrual basis and going concern and acknowledges the inherent constraint of benefit versus cost.
- *IFRS Financial Statements*: IAS No. 1 prescribes that a complete set of financial statements includes a statement of financial position (balance sheet), a statement of comprehensive income (either two statements—one for net income and one for comprehensive income—or a single statement combining both net income and comprehensive income), a statement of changes in equity, a cash flow statement, and notes. The notes include a summary of significant accounting policies and other explanatory information.
  - Financial statements need to reflect certain basic features: fair presentation, going concern, accrual basis, materiality and aggregation, no offsetting, and consistency.

---

[1] *Conceptual Framework for Financial Reporting (2010)*, International Accounting Standards Board, 2010, Chapter 1, OB2.

- Financial statements must be prepared at least annually and must include comparative information from the previous period.
- Financial statements must follow certain presentation requirements including a classified balance sheet, minimum information on the face of the financial statements and in the notes.
- *Characteristics of a Coherent Financial Reporting Framework*: Effective frameworks share three characteristics: transparency, comprehensiveness, and consistency. Effective standards can, however, differ on appropriate valuation bases, the basis for standard setting (principle or rules based), and resolution of conflicts between balance sheet and income statement focus.
- *Comparison of IFRS with Alternative Reporting Systems*: A significant number of the world's listed companies report under either IFRS or US GAAP.
  - Although these standards are moving toward convergence, there are still significant differences in the framework and individual standards.
  - In most cases, a user of financial statements will lack the information necessary to make specific adjustments required to achieve comparability between companies that use IFRS and companies that use US GAAP. Instead, an analyst must maintain general caution in interpreting comparative financial measures produced under different accounting standards and monitor significant developments in financial reporting standards.
- *Monitoring Developments*: Analysts can remain aware of ongoing developments in financial reporting by monitoring three areas: new products or types of transactions; actions of standard setters, regulators, and other groups; and company disclosures regarding critical accounting policies and estimates.

PROBLEMS

1. Which of the following is *most likely* not an objective of financial statements?
   A. To provide information about the performance of an entity.
   B. To provide information about the financial position of an entity.
   C. To provide information about the users of an entity's financial statements.

2. International financial reporting standards are currently developed by which entity?
   A. The IFRS Foundation.
   B. The International Accounting Standards Board.
   C. The International Organization of Securities Commissions.

3. US generally accepted accounting principles are currently developed by which entity?
   A. The Securities and Exchange Commission.
   B. The Financial Accounting Standards Board.
   C. The Public Company Accounting Oversight Board.

4. Which of the following statements about desirable attributes of accounting standards boards is *most* accurate? Accounting standards boards should:
   A. concede to political pressures.
   B. be guided by a well articulated framework.
   C. be adequately funded by companies to which the standards apply.

5. A core objective of the International Organization of Securities Commissions is to:
   A. eliminate systematic risk.
   B. protect users of financial statements.
   C. ensure that markets are fair, efficient, and transparent.

6. According to the *Conceptual Framework for Financial Reporting (2010)*, which of the following is *not* an enhancing qualitative characteristic of information in financial statements?
   A. Accuracy.
   B. Timeliness.
   C. Comparability.

7. Which of the following is *not* a constraint on the financial statements according to the *Conceptual Framework (2010)*?
   A. Understandability.
   B. Benefit versus cost.
   C. Balancing of qualitative characteristics.

8. The assumption that an entity will continue to operate for the foreseeable future is called:
   A. accrual basis.
   B. comparability.
   C. going concern.

9. The assumption that the effects of transactions and other events are recognized when they occur, not when the cash flows occur, is called:
   A. relevance.
   B. accrual basis.
   C. going concern.

10. Neutrality of information in the financial statements most closely contributes to which qualitative characteristic?
    A. Relevance.
    B. Understandability.
    C. Faithful representation.

11. Valuing assets at the amount of cash or equivalents paid or the fair value of the consideration given to acquire them at the time of acquisition most closely describes which measurement of financial statement elements?
    A. Current cost.
    B. Historical cost.
    C. Realizable value.

12. The valuation technique under which assets are recorded at the amount that would be received in an orderly disposal is:
    A. current cost.
    B. present value.
    C. realizable value.

13. Which of the following is *not* a required financial statement according to IAS No. 1?
    A. Statement of financial position.
    B. Statement of changes in income.
    C. Statement of comprehensive income.

14. Which of the following elements of financial statements is *most* closely related to measurement of performance?
    A. Assets.
    B. Expenses.
    C. Liabilities.

15. Which of the following elements of financial statements is *most* closely related to measurement of financial position?
    A. Equity.
    B. Income.
    C. Expenses.

16. Which of the following is *not* a characteristic of a coherent financial reporting framework?
    A. Timeliness.
    B. Consistency.
    C. Transparency.

17. Which of the following is *not* a recognized approach to standard-setting?
    A. A rules-based approach.
    B. An asset/liability approach.
    C. A principles-based approach.

18. Which of the following disclosures regarding new accounting standards provides the *most* meaningful information to an analyst?
    A. The impact of adoption is discussed.
    B. The standard will have no material impact.
    C. Management is still evaluating the impact.

CHAPTER 4

UNDERSTANDING INCOME STATEMENTS

LEARNING OUTCOMES

After completing this chapter, you will be able to do the following:

- describe the components of the income statement and alternative presentation formats of that statement;
- describe general principles of revenue recognition and accrual accounting, specific revenue recognition applications (including accounting for long-term contracts, installment sales, barter transactions, gross and net reporting of revenue), and implications of revenue recognition principles for financial analysis;
- calculate revenue given information that might influence the choice of revenue recognition method;
- describe general principles of expense recognition, specific expense recognition applications, and implications of expense recognition choices for financial analysis;
- describe the financial reporting treatment and analysis of non-recurring items (including discontinued operations, extraordinary items, unusual or infrequent items) and changes in accounting standards;
- distinguish between the operating and non-operating components of the income statement;
- describe how earnings per share is calculated and calculate and interpret a company's earnings per share (both basic and diluted earnings per share) for both simple and complex capital structures;
- distinguish between dilutive and antidilutive securities, and describe the implications of each for the earnings per share calculation;
- convert income statements to common-size income statements;
- evaluate a company's financial performance using common-size income statements and financial ratios based on the income statement;
- describe, calculate, and interpret comprehensive income;
- describe other comprehensive income, and identify major types of items included in it.

SUMMARY OVERVIEW

- The income statement presents revenue, expenses, and net income.
- The components of the income statement include: revenue; cost of sales; sales, general, and administrative expenses; other operating expenses; non-operating income and expenses; gains and losses; non-recurring items; net income; and EPS.
- An income statement that presents a subtotal for gross profit (revenue minus cost of goods sold) is said to be presented in a multi-step format. One that does not present this subtotal is said to be presented in a single-step format.
- Revenue is recognized in the period it is earned, which may or may not be in the same period as the related cash collection. Recognition of revenue when earned is a fundamental principal of accrual accounting.
- In limited circumstances, specific revenue recognition methods may be applicable, including percentage of completion, completed contract, installment sales, and cost recovery.
- An analyst should identify differences in companies' revenue recognition methods and adjust reported revenue where possible to facilitate comparability. Where the available information does not permit adjustment, an analyst can characterize the revenue recognition as more or less conservative and thus qualitatively assess how differences in policies might affect financial ratios and judgments about profitability.
- The general principles of expense recognition include a process to match expenses either to revenue (such as, cost of goods sold) or to the time period in which the expenditure occurs (period costs such as, administrative salaries) or to the time period of expected benefits of the expenditures (such as, depreciation).
- In expense recognition, choice of method (i.e., depreciation method and inventory cost method), as well as estimates (i.e., uncollectible accounts, warranty expenses, assets' useful life, and salvage value) affect a company's reported income. An analyst should identify differences in companies' expense recognition methods and adjust reported financial statements where possible to facilitate comparability. Where the available information does not permit adjustment, an analyst can characterize the policies and estimates as more or less conservative and thus qualitatively assess how differences in policies might affect financial ratios and judgments about companies' performance.
- To assess a company's future earnings, it is helpful to separate those prior years' items of income and expense that are likely to continue in the future from those items that are less likely to continue.
- Under IFRS, a company should present additional line items, headings, and subtotals beyond those specified when such presentation is relevant to an understanding of the entity's financial performance. Some items from prior years clearly are not expected to continue in future periods and are separately disclosed on a company's income statement. Under US GAAP, two such items are specified 1) discontinued operations and 2) extraordinary items (IFRS prohibit reporting any item of income or expense as extraordinary). Both of these items are required to be reported separately from continuing operations, under US GAAP.
- For other items on a company's income statement, such as unusual items and accounting changes, the likelihood of their continuing in the future is somewhat less clear and requires the analyst to make some judgments.
- Non-operating items are reported separately from operating items on the income statement.

- Basic EPS is the amount of income available to common shareholders divided by the weighted average number of common shares outstanding over a period. The amount of income available to common shareholders is the amount of net income remaining after preferred dividends (if any) have been paid.
- If a company has a simple capital structure (i.e., one with no potentially dilutive securities), then its basic EPS is equal to its diluted EPS. If, however, a company has dilutive securities, its diluted EPS is lower than its basic EPS.
- Diluted EPS is calculated using the if-converted method for convertible securities and the treasury stock method for options.
- Common-size analysis of the income statement involves stating each line item on the income statement as a percentage of sales. Common-size statements facilitate comparison across time periods and across companies of different sizes.
- Two income-statement-based indicators of profitability are net profit margin and gross profit margin.
- Comprehensive income includes *both* net income and other revenue and expense items that are excluded from the net income calculation.

PROBLEMS

1. Expenses on the income statement may be grouped by:
   A. nature, but not by function.
   B. function, but not by nature.
   C. either function or nature.

2. An example of an expense classification by function is:
   A. tax expense.
   B. interest expense.
   C. cost of goods sold.

3. Denali Limited, a manufacturing company, had the following income statement information:

Revenue	$4,000,000
Cost of goods sold	$3,000,000
Other operating expenses	$ 500,000
Interest expense	$ 100,000
Tax expense	$ 120,000

   Denali's gross profit is equal to
   A. $280,000.
   B. $500,000.
   C. $1,000,000.

4. Under IFRS, income includes increases in economic benefits from:
   A. increases in liabilities not related to owners' contributions.
   B. enhancements of assets not related to owners' contributions.
   C. increases in owners' equity related to owners' contributions.

5. Fairplay had the following information related to the sale of its products during 2009, which was its first year of business:

Revenue	$1,000,000
Returns of goods sold	$ 100,000
Cash collected	$ 800,000
Cost of goods sold	$ 700,000

Under the accrual basis of accounting, how much net revenue would be reported on Fairplay's 2009 income statement?
   A. $200,000.
   B. $900,000.
   C. $1,000,000.

6. If the outcome of a long-term contract can be measured reliably, the preferred accounting method under both IFRS and US GAAP is:
   A. the cost recovery method.
   B. the completed contract method.
   C. the percentage-of-completion method.

7. At the beginning of 2009, Florida Road Construction entered into a contract to build a road for the government. Construction will take four years. The following information as of 31 December 2009 is available for the contract:

Total revenue according to contract	$10,000,000
Total expected cost	$ 8,000,000
Cost incurred during 2009	$ 1,200,000

Assume that the company estimates percentage complete based on costs incurred as a percentage of total estimated costs. Under the completed contract method, how much revenue will be reported in 2009?
   A. None.
   B. $300,000.
   C. $1,500,000.

8. During 2009, Argo Company sold 10 acres of prime commercial zoned land to a builder for $5,000,000. The builder gave Argo a $1,000,000 down payment and will pay the remaining balance of $4,000,000 to Argo in 2010. Argo purchased the land in 2002 for $2,000,000. Using the installment method, how much profit will Argo report for 2009?
   A. $600,000.
   B. $1,000,000.
   C. $3,000,000.

9. Using the same information as in Question 8, how much profit will Argo report for 2009 using the cost recovery method?
   A. None.
   B. $600,000.
   C. $1,000,000.

10. Under IFRS, revenue from barter transactions should be measured based on the fair value of revenue from:
    A. similar barter transactions with unrelated parties.
    B. similar non-barter transactions with related parties.
    C. similar non-barter transactions with unrelated parties.

11. Apex Consignment sells items over the internet for individuals on a consignment basis. Apex receives the items from the owner, lists them for sale on the internet, and receives a 25 percent commission for any items sold. Apex collects the full amount from the buyer and pays the net amount after commission to the owner. Unsold items are returned to the owner after 90 days. During 2009, Apex had the following information:
    • Total sales price of items sold during 2009 on consignment was €2,000,000.
    • Total commissions retained by Apex during 2009 for these items was €500,000.
    How much revenue should Apex report on its 2009 income statement?
    A. €500,000.
    B. €2,000,000.
    C. €1,500,000.

12. During 2009, Accent Toys Plc., which began business in October of that year, purchased 10,000 units of a toy at a cost of £10 per unit in October. The toy sold well in October. In anticipation of heavy December sales, Accent purchased 5,000 additional units in November at a cost of £11 per unit. During 2009, Accent sold 12,000 units at a price of £15 per unit. Under the first in, first out (FIFO) method, what is Accent's cost of goods sold for 2009?
    A. £120,000.
    B. £122,000.
    C. £124,000.

13. Using the same information as in Question 12, what would Accent's cost of goods sold be under the weighted average cost method?
    A. £120,000.
    B. £122,000.
    C. £124,000.

14. Which inventory method is least likely to be used under IFRS?
    A. First in, first out (FIFO).
    B. Last in, first out (LIFO).
    C. Weighted average.

15. At the beginning of 2009, Glass Manufacturing purchased a new machine for its assembly line at a cost of $600,000. The machine has an estimated useful life of 10 years and estimated residual value of $50,000. Under the straight-line method, how much depreciation would Glass take in 2010 for financial reporting purposes?
    A. $55,000.
    B. $60,000.
    C. $65,000.

16. Using the same information as in Question 15, how much depreciation would Glass take in 2009 for financial reporting purposes under the double-declining balance method?
    A. $60,000.
    B. $110,000.
    C. $120,000.

17. Which combination of depreciation methods and useful lives is most conservative in the year a depreciable asset is acquired?
    A. Straight-line depreciation with a short useful life.
    B. Declining balance depreciation with a long useful life.
    C. Declining balance depreciation with a short useful life.

18. Under IFRS, a loss from the destruction of property in a fire would most likely be classified as:
    A. an extraordinary item.
    B. continuing operations.
    C. discontinued operations.

19. For 2009, Flamingo Products had net income of $1,000,000. At 1 January 2009, there were 1,000,000 shares outstanding. On 1 July 2009, the company issued 100,000 new shares for $20 per share. The company paid $200,000 in dividends to common shareholders. What is Flamingo's basic earnings per share for 2009?
    A. $0.80.
    B. $0.91.
    C. $0.95.

20. Cell Services Inc. (CSI) had 1,000,000 average shares outstanding during all of 2009. During 2009, CSI also had 10,000 options outstanding with exercise prices of $10 each. The average stock price of CSI during 2009 was $15. For purposes of computing diluted earnings per share, how many shares would be used in the denominator?
    A. 1,003,333.
    B. 1,006,667.
    C. 1,010,000.

CHAPTER 5

UNDERSTANDING BALANCE SHEETS

LEARNING OUTCOMES

After completing this chapter, you will be able to do the following:

- describe the elements of the balance sheet: assets, liabilities, and equity;
- describe uses and limitations of the balance sheet in financial analysis;
- describe alternative formats of balance sheet presentation;
- distinguish between current and non-current assets, and current and non-current liabilities;
- describe different types of assets and liabilities and the measurement bases of each;
- describe the components of shareholders' equity;
- convert balance sheets to common-size balance sheets and interpret common-size balance sheets;
- calculate and interpret liquidity and solvency ratios.

SUMMARY OVERVIEW

- The balance sheet distinguishes between current and non-current assets and between current and non-current liabilities unless a presentation based on liquidity provides more relevant and reliable information.
- The concept of liquidity relates to a company's ability to pay for its near-term operating needs. With respect to a company overall, liquidity refers to the availability of cash to pay those near-term needs. With respect to a particular asset or liability, liquidity refers to its "nearness to cash."
- Some assets and liabilities are measured on the basis of fair value and some are measured at historical cost. Notes to financial statements provide information that is helpful in assessing the comparability of measurement bases across companies.

- Assets expected to be liquidated or used up within one year or one operating cycle of the business, whichever is greater, are classified as current assets. Assets not expected to be liquidated or used up within one year or one operating cycle of the business, whichever is greater, are classified as non-current assets.
- Liabilities expected to be settled or paid within one year or one operating cycle of the business, whichever is greater, are classified as current liabilities. Liabilities not expected to be settled or paid within one year or one operating cycle of the business, whichever is greater, are classified as non-current liabilities.
- Trade receivables, also referred to as accounts receivable, are amounts owed to a company by its customers for products and services already delivered. Receivables are reported net of the allowance for doubtful accounts.
- Inventories are physical products that will eventually be sold to the company's customers, either in their current form (finished goods) or as inputs into a process to manufacture a final product (raw materials and work-in-process). Inventories are reported at the lower of cost or net realizable value. If the net realizable value of a company's inventory falls below its carrying amount, the company must write down the value of the inventory and record an expense.
- Inventory cost is based on specific identification or estimated using the first-in, first-out or weighted average cost methods. Some accounting standards (including US GAAP but not IFRS) also allow last-in, first-out as an additional inventory valuation method.
- Accounts payable, also called trade payables, are amounts that a business owes its vendors for purchases of goods and services.
- Deferred revenue (also known as unearned revenue) arises when a company receives payment in advance of delivery of the goods and services associated with the payment received.
- Property, plant, and equipment (PPE) are tangible assets that are used in company operations and expected to be used over more than one fiscal period. Examples of tangible assets include land, buildings, equipment, machinery, furniture, and natural resources such as mineral and petroleum resources.
- IFRS provide companies with the choice to report PPE using either a historical cost model or a revaluation model. US GAAP permit only the historical cost model for reporting PPE.
- Depreciation is the process of recognizing the cost of a long-lived asset over its useful life. (Land is not depreciated.)
- Under IFRS, property used to earn rental income or capital appreciation is considered to be investment property. IFRS provide companies with the choice to report investment property using either a historical cost model or a fair value model.
- Intangible assets refer to identifiable non-monetary assets without physical substance. Examples include patents, licenses, and trademarks. For each intangible asset, a company assesses whether the useful life is finite or indefinite.
- An intangible asset with a finite useful life is amortised on a systematic basis over the best estimate of its useful life, with the amortisation method and useful-life estimate reviewed at least annually. Impairment principles for an intangible asset with a finite useful life are the same as for PPE.
- An intangible asset with an indefinite useful life is not amortised. Instead, it is tested for impairment at least annually.
- For internally generated intangible assets, IFRS require that costs incurred during the research phase must be expensed. Costs incurred in the development stage can be capitalized as intangible assets if certain criteria are met, including technological feasibility, the ability to use or sell the resulting asset, and the ability to complete the project.

- The most common asset that is not a separately identifiable asset is goodwill, which arises in business combinations. Goodwill is not amortised; instead it is tested for impairment at least annually.
- Financial instruments are contracts that give rise to both a financial asset of one entity and a financial liability or equity instrument of another entity. In general, there are two basic alternative ways that financial instruments are measured: fair value or amortised cost. For financial instruments measured at fair value, there are two basic alternatives in how net changes in fair value are recognized: as profit or loss on the income statement, or as other comprehensive income (loss) which bypasses the income statement.
- Typical long-term financial liabilities include loans (i.e., borrowings from banks) and notes or bonds payable (i.e., fixed-income securities issued to investors). Liabilities such as bonds issued by a company are usually reported at amortised cost on the balance sheet.
- Deferred tax liabilities arise from temporary timing differences between a company's income as reported for tax purposes and income as reported for financial statement purposes.
- Six potential components that comprise the owners' equity section of the balance sheet include: contributed capital, preferred shares, treasury shares, retained earnings, accumulated other comprehensive income, and non-controlling interest.
- The statement of changes in equity reflects information about the increases or decreases in each component of a company's equity over a period.
- Vertical common-size analysis of the balance sheet involves stating each balance sheet item as a percentage of total assets.
- Balance sheet ratios include liquidity ratios (measuring the company's ability to meet its short-term obligations) and solvency ratios (measuring the company's ability to meet long-term and other obligations).

PROBLEMS

1. Resources controlled by a company as a result of past events are:
   A. equity.
   B. assets.
   C. liabilities.

2. Equity equals:
   A. Assets – Liabilities.
   B. Liabilities – Assets.
   C. Assets + Liabilities.

3. Distinguishing between current and non-current items on the balance sheet and presenting a subtotal for current assets and liabilities is referred to as:
   A. a classified balance sheet.
   B. an unclassified balance sheet.
   C. a liquidity-based balance sheet.

4. All of the following are current assets *except*:
   A. cash.
   B. goodwill.
   C. inventories.

5. Debt due within one year is considered:
   A. current.
   B. preferred.
   C. convertible.

6. Money received from customers for products to be delivered in the future is recorded as:
   A. revenue and an asset.
   B. an asset and a liability.
   C. revenue and a liability.

7. The carrying value of inventories reflects:
   A. their historical cost.
   B. their current value.
   C. the lower of historical cost or net realizable value.

8. When a company pays its rent in advance, its balance sheet will reflect a reduction in:
   A. assets and liabilities.
   B. assets and shareholders' equity.
   C. one category of assets and an increase in another.

9. Accrued expenses (accrued liabilities) are:
   A. expenses that have been paid.
   B. created when another liability is reduced.
   C. expenses that have been reported on the income statement but not yet paid.

10. The initial measurement of goodwill is *most likely* affected by:
    A. an acquisition's purchase price.
    B. the acquired company's book value.
    C. the fair value of the acquirer's assets and liabilities.

11. Defining total asset turnover as revenue divided by average total assets, all else equal, impairment write-downs of long-lived assets owned by a company will *most likely* result in an increase for that company in:
    A. the debt-to-equity ratio but not the total asset turnover.
    B. the total asset turnover but not the debt-to-equity ratio.
    C. both the debt-to-equity ratio and the total asset turnover.

12. For financial assets classified as trading securities, how are unrealized gains and losses reflected in shareholders' equity?
    A. They are not recognized.
    B. They flow through income into retained earnings.
    C. They are a component of accumulated other comprehensive income.

13. For financial assets classified as available for sale, how are unrealized gains and losses reflected in shareholders' equity?
    A. They are not recognized.
    B. They flow through retained earnings.
    C. They are a component of accumulated other comprehensive income.

14. For financial assets classified as held to maturity, how are unrealized gains and losses reflected in shareholders' equity?
    A. They are not recognized.
    B. They flow through retained earnings.
    C. They are a component of accumulated other comprehensive income.

15. The non-controlling (minority) interest in consolidated subsidiaries is presented on the balance sheet:
    A. as a long-term liability.
    B. separately, but as a part of shareholders' equity.
    C. as a mezzanine item between liabilities and shareholders' equity.

16. The item "retained earnings" is a component of:
    A. assets.
    B. liabilities.
    C. shareholders' equity.

17. When a company buys shares of its own stock to be held in treasury, it records a reduction in:
    A. both assets and liabilities.
    B. both assets and shareholders' equity.
    C. assets and an increase in shareholders' equity.

18. Which of the following would an analyst *most likely* be able to determine from a common-size analysis of a company's balance sheet over several periods?
    A. An increase or decrease in sales.
    B. An increase or decrease in financial leverage.
    C. A more efficient or less efficient use of assets.

19. An investor concerned whether a company can meet its near-term obligations is *most likely* to calculate the:
    A. current ratio.
    B. return on total capital.
    C. financial leverage ratio.

20. The most stringent test of a company's liquidity is its:
    A. cash ratio.
    B. quick ratio.
    C. current ratio.

21. An investor worried about a company's long-term solvency would *most likely* examine its:
    A. current ratio.
    B. return on equity.
    C. debt-to-equity ratio.

22. Using the information presented in Exhibit 4, the quick ratio for SAP Group at 31 December 2009 is *closest* to:
    A. 1.01.
    B. 1.44.
    C. 1.54.

23. Using the information presented in Exhibit 12, the financial leverage ratio for SAP Group at 31 December 2009 is *closest* to:
    A. 0.08.
    B. 0.58.
    C. 1.58.

CHAPTER 6

UNDERSTANDING CASH FLOW STATEMENTS

LEARNING OUTCOMES

After completing this chapter, you will be able to do the following:

- compare cash flows from operating, investing, and financing activities and classify cash flow items as relating to one of those three categories given a description of the items;
- describe how non-cash investing and financing activities are reported;
- contrast cash flow statements prepared under International Financial Reporting Standards (IFRS) and US generally accepted accounting principles (US GAAP);
- distinguish between the direct and indirect methods of presenting cash from operating activities and describe arguments in favor of each method;
- describe how the cash flow statement is linked to the income statement and the balance sheet;
- describe the steps in the preparation of direct and indirect cash flow statements, including how cash flows can be computed using income statement and balance sheet data;
- convert cash flows from the indirect to direct method;
- analyze and interpret both reported and common-size cash flow statements;
- calculate and interpret free cash flow to the firm, free cash flow to equity, and performance and coverage cash flow ratios.

SUMMARY OVERVIEW

- Cash flow activities are classified into three categories: operating activities, investing activities, and financing activities. Significant non-cash transaction activities (if present) are reported by using a supplemental disclosure note to the cash flow statement.

- Cash flow statements under IFRS and US GAAP are similar; however, IFRS provide companies with more choices in classifying some cash flow items as operating, investing, or financing activities.
- Companies can use either the direct or the indirect method for reporting their operating cash flow:
  - The direct method discloses operating cash inflows by source (e.g., cash received from customers, cash received from investment income) and operating cash outflows by use (e.g., cash paid to suppliers, cash paid for interest) in the operating activities section of the cash flow statement.
  - The indirect method reconciles net income to operating cash flow by adjusting net income for all non-cash items and the net changes in the operating working capital accounts.
- The cash flow statement is linked to a company's income statement and comparative balance sheets and to data on those statements.
- Although the indirect method is most commonly used by companies, an analyst can generally convert it to an approximation of the direct format by following a simple three-step process.
- An evaluation of a cash flow statement should involve an assessment of the sources and uses of cash and the main drivers of cash flow within each category of activities.
- The analyst can use common-size statement analysis for the cash flow statement. Two approaches to developing the common-size statements are the total cash inflows/total cash outflows method and the percentage of net revenues method.
- The cash flow statement can be used to determine free cash flow to the firm (FCFF) and free cash flow to equity (FCFE).
- The cash flow statement may also be used in financial ratios that measure a company's profitability, performance, and financial strength.

PROBLEMS

1. The three major classifications of activities in a cash flow statement are:
   A. inflows, outflows, and net flows.
   B. operating, investing, and financing.
   C. revenues, expenses, and net income.

2. The sale of a building for cash would be classified as what type of activity on the cash flow statement?
   A. Operating.
   B. Investing.
   C. Financing.

3. Which of the following is an example of a financing activity on the cash flow statement under US GAAP?
   A. Payment of interest.
   B. Receipt of dividends.
   C. Payment of dividends.

4. A conversion of a face value $1 million convertible bond for $1 million of common stock would most likely be:
   A. reported as a $1 million investing cash inflow and outflow.
   B. reported as a $1 million financing cash outflow and inflow.
   C. reported as supplementary information to the cash flow statement.

5. Interest paid is classified as an operating cash flow under:
   A. US GAAP but may be classified as either operating or investing cash flows under IFRS.
   B. IFRS but may be classified as either operating or investing cash flows under US GAAP.
   C. US GAAP but may be classified as either operating or financing cash flows under IFRS.

6. Cash flows from taxes on income must be separately disclosed under:
   A. IFRS only.
   B. US GAAP only.
   C. both IFRS and US GAAP.

7. Which of the following components of the cash flow statement may be prepared under the indirect method under both IFRS and US GAAP?
   A. Operating.
   B. Investing.
   C. Financing.

8. Which of the following is *most likely* to appear in the operating section of a cash flow statement under the indirect method?
   A. Net income.
   B. Cash paid to suppliers.
   C. Cash received from customers.

9. Red Road Company, a consulting company, reported total revenues of $100 million, total expenses of $80 million, and net income of $20 million in the most recent year. If accounts receivable increased by $10 million, how much cash did the company receive from customers?
   A. $90 million.
   B. $100 million.
   C. $110 million.

10. Green Glory Corp., a garden supply wholesaler, reported cost of goods sold for the year of $80 million. Total assets increased by $55 million, including an increase of $5 million in inventory. Total liabilities increased by $45 million, including an increase of $2 million in accounts payable. The cash paid by the company to its suppliers is most likely *closest* to:
    A. $73 million.
    B. $77 million.
    C. $83 million.

11. Purple Fleur S.A., a retailer of floral products, reported cost of goods sold for the year of $75 million. Total assets increased by $55 million, but inventory declined by $6 million. Total liabilities increased by $45 million, and accounts payable increased by $2 million. The cash paid by the company to its suppliers is most likely *closest* to:
    A. $67 million.
    B. $79 million.
    C. $83 million.

12. White Flag, a women's clothing manufacturer, reported salaries expense of $20 million. The beginning balance of salaries payable was $3 million, and the ending balance of salaries payable was $1 million. How much cash did the company pay in salaries?
    A. $18 million.
    B. $21 million.
    C. $22 million.

13. An analyst gathered the following information from a company's 2010 financial statements (in $ millions):

Year ended 31 December	2009	2010
Net sales	245.8	254.6
Cost of goods sold	168.3	175.9
Accounts receivable	73.2	68.3
Inventory	39.0	47.8
Accounts payable	20.3	22.9

Based only on the information above, the company's 2010 statement of cash flows in the direct format would include amounts (in $ millions) for cash received from customers and cash paid to suppliers, respectively, that are *closest* to:

	Cash Received from Customers	Cash Paid to Suppliers
A.	249.7	169.7
B.	259.5	174.5
C.	259.5	182.1

14. Golden Cumulus Corp., a commodities trading company, reported interest expense of $19 million and taxes of $6 million. Interest payable increased by $3 million, and taxes payable decreased by $4 million over the period. How much cash did the company pay for interest and taxes?
    A. $22 million for interest and $10 million for taxes.
    B. $16 million for interest and $2 million for taxes.
    C. $16 million for interest and $10 million for taxes.

15. An analyst gathered the following information from a company's 2010 financial statements (in $ millions):

Balances as of Year Ended 31 December	2009	2010
Retained earnings	120	145
Accounts receivable	38	43
Inventory	45	48
Accounts payable	36	29

In 2010, the company declared and paid cash dividends of $10 million and recorded depreciation expense in the amount of $25 million. The company considers dividends paid a financing activity. The company's 2010 cash flow from operations (in $ millions) was *closest* to
    A. 25.
    B. 45.
    C. 75.

16. Silverago Incorporated, an international metals company, reported a loss on the sale of equipment of $2 million in 2010. In addition, the company's income statement shows depreciation expense of $8 million and the cash flow statement shows capital expenditure of $10 million, all of which was for the purchase of new equipment. Using the following information from the comparative balance sheets, how much cash did the company receive from the equipment sale?

Balance Sheet Item	12/31/2009	12/31/2010	Change
Equipment	$100 million	$105 million	$5 million
Accumulated depreciation—equipment	$40 million	$46 million	$6 million

   A. $1 million.
   B. $2 million.
   C. $3 million.

17. Jaderong Plinkett Stores reported net income of $25 million. The company has no outstanding debt. Using the following information from the comparative balance sheets (in millions), what should the company report in the financing section of the statement of cash flows in 2010?

Balance Sheet Item	12/31/2009	12/31/2010	Change
Common stock	$100	$102	$ 2
Additional paid-in capital common stock	$100	$140	$40
Retained earnings	$100	$115	$15
Total stockholders' equity	$300	$357	$57

   A. Issuance of common stock of $42 million; dividends paid of $10 million.
   B. Issuance of common stock of $38 million; dividends paid of $10 million.
   C. Issuance of common stock of $42 million; dividends paid of $40 million.

18. Based on the following information for Star Inc., what are the total net adjustments that the company would make to net income in order to derive operating cash flow?

Income Statement Item		Year Ended 12/31/2010
Net income		$20 million
Depreciation		$ 2 million

Balance Sheet Item	12/31/2009	12/31/2010	Change
Accounts receivable	$25 million	$22 million	($3 million)
Inventory	$10 million	$14 million	$4 million
Accounts payable	$ 8 million	$13 million	$5 million

   A. Add $2 million.
   B. Add $6 million.
   C. Subtract $6 million.

19. The first step in cash flow statement analysis should be to:
   A. evaluate consistency of cash flows.
   B. determine operating cash flow drivers.
   C. identify the major sources and uses of cash.

20. Which of the following would be valid conclusions from an analysis of the cash flow statement for Telefónica Group presented in Exhibit 3?
    A. The primary use of cash is financing activities.
    B. The primary source of cash is operating activities.
    C. Telefónica classifies interest received as an operating activity.

21. Which is an appropriate method of preparing a common-size cash flow statement?
    A. Show each item of revenue and expense as a percentage of net revenue.
    B. Show each line item on the cash flow statement as a percentage of net revenue.
    C. Show each line item on the cash flow statement as a percentage of total cash outflows.

22. Which of the following is an appropriate method of computing free cash flow to the firm?
    A. Add operating cash flows to capital expenditures and deduct after-tax interest payments.
    B. Add operating cash flows to after-tax interest payments and deduct capital expenditures.
    C. Deduct both after-tax interest payments and capital expenditures from operating cash flows.

23. An analyst has calculated a ratio using as the numerator the sum of operating cash flow, interest, and taxes and as the denominator the amount of interest. What is this ratio, what does it measure, and what does it indicate?
    A. This ratio is an interest coverage ratio, measuring a company's ability to meet its interest obligations and indicating a company's solvency.
    B. This ratio is an effective tax ratio, measuring the amount of a company's operating cash flow used for taxes and indicating a company's efficiency in tax management.
    C. This ratio is an operating profitability ratio, measuring the operating cash flow generated accounting for taxes and interest and indicating a company's liquidity.

CHAPTER 7

FINANCIAL ANALYSIS TECHNIQUES

LEARNING OUTCOMES

After completing this chapter, you will be able to do the following:

- describe tools and techniques used in financial analysis, including their uses and limitations;
- classify, calculate, and interpret activity, liquidity, solvency, profitability, and valuation ratios;
- describe relationships among ratios and evaluate a company using ratio analysis;
- demonstrate the application of DuPont analysis of return on equity, and calculate and interpret effects of changes in its components;
- calculate and interpret ratios used in equity analysis and credit analysis;
- explain the requirements for segment reporting, and calculate and interpret segment ratios;
- describe how ratio analysis and other techniques can be used to model and forecast earnings.

SUMMARY OVERVIEW

- Common-size financial statements and financial ratios remove the effect of size, allowing comparisons of a company with peer companies (cross-sectional analysis) and comparison of a company's results over time (trend or time-series analysis).
- Activity ratios measure the efficiency of a company's operations, such as collection of receivables or management of inventory. Major activity ratios include inventory turnover, days of inventory on hand, receivables turnover, days of sales outstanding, payables turnover, number of days of payables, working capital turnover, fixed asset turnover, and total asset turnover.
- Liquidity ratios measure the ability of a company to meet short-term obligations. Major liquidity ratios include the current ratio, quick ratio, cash ratio, and defensive interval ratio.

- Solvency ratios measure the ability of a company to meet long-term obligations. Major solvency ratios include debt ratios (including the debt-to-assets ratio, debt-to-capital ratio, debt-to-equity ratio, and financial leverage ratio) and coverage ratios (including interest coverage and fixed charge coverage).
- Profitability ratios measure the ability of a company to generate profits from revenue and assets. Major profitability ratios include return on sales ratios (including gross profit margin, operating profit margin, pretax margin, and net profit margin) and return on investment ratios (including operating ROA, ROA, return on total capital, ROE, and return on common equity).
- Ratios can also be combined and evaluated as a group to better understand how they fit together and how efficiency and leverage are tied to profitability.
- ROE can be analyzed as the product of the net profit margin, asset turnover, and financial leverage. This decomposition is sometimes referred to as DuPont analysis.
- Valuation ratios express the relation between the market value of a company or its equity (for example, price per share) and some fundamental financial metric (for example, earnings per share).
- Ratio analysis is useful in the selection and valuation of debt and equity securities and is a part of the credit rating process.
- Ratios can also be computed for business segments to evaluate how units within a business are performing.
- The results of financial analysis provide valuable inputs into forecasts of future earnings and cash flow.

PROBLEMS

1. Comparison of a company's financial results to other peer companies for the same time period is called:
   A. technical analysis.
   B. time-series analysis.
   C. cross-sectional analysis.

2. In order to assess a company's ability to fulfill its long-term obligations, an analyst would *most likely* examine:
   A. activity ratios.
   B. liquidity ratios.
   C. solvency ratios.

3. Which ratio would a company *most likely* use to measure its ability to meet short-term obligations?
   A. Current ratio.
   B. Payables turnover.
   C. Gross profit margin.

4. Which of the following ratios would be *most* useful in determining a company's ability to cover its lease and interest payments?
   A. ROA.
   B. Total asset turnover.
   C. Fixed charge coverage.

5. An analyst is interested in assessing both the efficiency and liquidity of Spherion PLC. The analyst has collected the following data for Spherion:

	FY3	FY2	FY1
Days of inventory on hand	32	34	40
Days sales outstanding	28	25	23
Number of days of payables	40	35	35

Based on this data, what is the analyst *least likely* to conclude?
A. Inventory management has contributed to improved liquidity.
B. Management of payables has contributed to improved liquidity.
C. Management of receivables has contributed to improved liquidity.

6. An analyst is evaluating the solvency and liquidity of Apex Manufacturing and has collected the following data (in millions of euro):

	FY5 (€)	FY4 (€)	FY3 (€)
Total debt	2,000	1,900	1,750
Total equity	4,000	4,500	5,000

Which of the following would be the analyst's *most likely* conclusion?
A. The company is becoming increasingly less solvent, as evidenced by the increase in its debt-to-equity ratio from 0.35 to 0.50 from FY3 to FY5.
B. The company is becoming less liquid, as evidenced by the increase in its debt-to-equity ratio from 0.35 to 0.50 from FY3 to FY5.
C. The company is becoming increasingly more liquid, as evidenced by the increase in its debt-to-equity ratio from 0.35 to 0.50 from FY3 to FY5.

7. With regard to the data in Problem 6, what would be the *most* reasonable explanation of the financial data?
A. The decline in the company's equity results from a decline in the market value of this company's common shares.
B. The €250 increase in the company's debt from FY3 to FY5 indicates that lenders are viewing the company as increasingly creditworthy.
C. The decline in the company's equity indicates that the company may be incurring losses, paying dividends greater than income, and/or repurchasing shares.

8. An analyst observes a decrease in a company's inventory turnover. Which of the following would *most likely* explain this trend?
A. The company installed a new inventory management system, allowing more efficient inventory management.
B. Due to problems with obsolescent inventory last year, the company wrote off a large amount of its inventory at the beginning of the period.
C. The company installed a new inventory management system but experienced some operational difficulties resulting in duplicate orders being placed with suppliers.

9. Which of the following would *best* explain an increase in receivables turnover?
A. The company adopted new credit policies last year and began offering credit to customers with weak credit histories.

B. Due to problems with an error in its old credit scoring system, the company had accumulated a substantial amount of uncollectible accounts and wrote off a large amount of its receivables.

C. To match the terms offered by its closest competitor, the company adopted new payment terms now requiring net payment within 30 days rather than 15 days, which had been its previous requirement.

10. Brown Corporation had average days of sales outstanding of 19 days in the most recent fiscal year. Brown wants to improve its credit policies and collection practices and decrease its collection period in the next fiscal year to match the industry average of 15 days. Credit sales in the most recent fiscal year were $300 million, and Brown expects credit sales to increase to $390 million in the next fiscal year. To achieve Brown's goal of decreasing the collection period, the change in the average accounts receivable balance that must occur is *closest* to:

A. +$0.41 million.

B. –$0.41 million.

C. –$1.22 million.

11. An analyst observes the following data for two companies:

	Company A ($)	Company B ($)
Revenue	4,500	6,000
Net income	50	1,000
Current assets	40,000	60,000
Total assets	100,000	700,000
Current liabilities	10,000	50,000
Total debt	60,000	150,000
Shareholders' equity	30,000	500,000

Which of the following choices *best* describes reasonable conclusions that the analyst might make about the two companies' abilities to pay their current and long-term obligations?

A. Company A's current ratio of 4.0 indicates it is more liquid than Company B, whose current ratio is only 1.2, but Company B is more solvent, as indicated by its lower debt-to-equity ratio.

B. Company A's current ratio of 0.25 indicates it is less liquid than Company B, whose current ratio is 0.83, and Company A is also less solvent, as indicated by a debt-to-equity ratio of 200 percent compared with Company B's debt-to-equity ratio of only 30 percent.

C. Company A's current ratio of 4.0 indicates it is more liquid than Company B, whose current ratio is only 1.2, and Company A is also more solvent, as indicated by a debt-to-equity ratio of 200 percent compared with Company B's debt-to-equity ratio of only 30 percent.

The following information relates to Questions 12–15

The data in Exhibit 1 appear in the five-year summary of a major international company. A business combination with another major manufacturer took place in FY13.

EXHIBIT 1

	FY10	FY11	FY12	FY13	FY14
Financial statements	GBP m	GBP m	GBP m	GBP m	GBP m
Income statements					
Revenue	4,390	3,624	3,717	8,167	11,366
Profit before interest and taxation (EBIT)	844	700	704	933	1,579
Net interest payable	−80	−54	−98	−163	−188
Taxation	−186	−195	−208	−349	−579
Minorities	−94	−99	−105	−125	−167
Profit for the year	484	352	293	296	645
Balance sheets					
Fixed assets	3,510	3,667	4,758	10,431	11,483
Current asset investments, cash at bank and in hand	316	218	290	561	682
Other current assets	558	514	643	1,258	1,634
Total assets	4,384	4,399	5,691	12,250	13,799
Interest bearing debt (long term)	−602	−1,053	−1,535	−3,523	−3,707
Other creditors and provisions (current)	−1,223	−1,054	−1,102	−2,377	−3,108
Total liabilities	−1,825	−2,107	−2,637	−5,900	−6,815
Net assets	2,559	2,292	3,054	6,350	6,984
Shareholders' funds	2,161	2,006	2,309	5,572	6,165
Equity minority interests	398	286	745	778	819
Capital employed	2,559	2,292	3,054	6,350	6,984
Cash flow					
Working capital movements	−53	5	71	85	107
Net cash inflow from operating activities	864	859	975	1,568	2,292

12. The company's total assets at year-end FY9 were GBP 3,500 million. Which of the following choices *best* describes reasonable conclusions an analyst might make about the company's efficiency?

   A. Comparing FY14 with FY10, the company's efficiency improved, as indicated by a total asset turnover ratio of 0.86 compared with 0.64.

   B. Comparing FY14 with FY10, the company's efficiency deteriorated, as indicated by its current ratio.

   C. Comparing FY14 with FY10, the company's efficiency deteriorated due to asset growth faster than turnover revenue growth.

13. Which of the following choices *best* describes reasonable conclusions an analyst might make about the company's solvency?
    A. Comparing FY14 with FY10, the company's solvency improved, as indicated by an increase in its debt-to-assets ratio from 0.14 to 0.27.
    B. Comparing FY14 with FY10, the company's solvency deteriorated, as indicated by a decrease in interest coverage from 10.6 to 8.4.
    C. Comparing FY14 with FY10, the company's solvency improved, as indicated by the growth in its profits to GBP 645 million.

14. Which of the following choices *best* describes reasonable conclusions an analyst might make about the company's liquidity?
    A. Comparing FY14 with FY10, the company's liquidity improved, as indicated by an increase in its debt-to-assets ratio from 0.14 to 0.27.
    B. Comparing FY14 with FY10, the company's liquidity deteriorated, as indicated by a decrease in interest coverage from 10.6 to 8.4.
    C. Comparing FY14 with FY10, the company's liquidity improved, as indicated by an increase in its current ratio from 0.71 to 0.75.

15. Which of the following choices *best* describes reasonable conclusions an analyst might make about the company's profitability?
    A. Comparing FY14 with FY10, the company's profitability improved, as indicated by an increase in its debt-to-assets ratio from 0.14 to 0.27.
    B. Comparing FY14 with FY10, the company's profitability deteriorated, as indicated by a decrease in its net profit margin from 11.0 percent to 5.7 percent.
    C. Comparing FY14 with FY10, the company's profitability improved, as indicated by the growth in its shareholders' equity to GBP 6,165 million.

16. Assuming no changes in other variables, which of the following would decrease ROA?
    A. A decrease in the effective tax rate.
    B. A decrease in interest expense.
    C. An increase in average assets.

17. An analyst compiles the following data for a company:

	FY13	FY14	FY15
ROE	19.8%	20.0%	22.0%
Return on total assets	8.1%	8.0%	7.9%
Total asset turnover	2.0	2.0	2.1

Based only on the information above, the *most* appropriate conclusion is that, over the period FY13 to FY15, the company's:
A. net profit margin and financial leverage have decreased.
B. net profit margin and financial leverage have increased.
C. net profit margin has decreased but its financial leverage has increased.

18. A decomposition of ROE for Integra SA is as follows:

	FY12	FY11
ROE	18.90%	18.90%
Tax burden	0.70	0.75
Interest burden	0.90	0.90
EBIT margin	10.00%	10.00%
Asset turnover	1.50	1.40
Leverage	2.00	2.00

Which of the following choices *best* describes reasonable conclusions an analyst might make based on this ROE decomposition?

A. Profitability and the liquidity position both improved in FY12.

B. The higher average tax rate in FY12 offset the improvement in profitability, leaving ROE unchanged.

C. The higher average tax rate in FY12 offset the improvement in efficiency, leaving ROE unchanged.

19. A decomposition of ROE for Company A and Company B is as follows:

	Company A		Company B	
	FY15	FY14	FY15	FY14
ROE	26.46%	18.90%	26.33%	18.90%
Tax burden	0.7	0.75	0.75	0.75
Interest burden	0.9	0.9	0.9	0.9
EBIT margin	7.00%	10.00%	13.00%	10.00%
Asset turnover	1.5	1.4	1.5	1.4
Leverage	4	2	2	2

An analyst is *most likely* to conclude that:

A. Company A's ROE is higher than Company B's in FY15, and one explanation consistent with the data is that Company A may have purchased new, more efficient equipment.

B. Company A's ROE is higher than Company B's in FY15, and one explanation consistent with the data is that Company A has made a strategic shift to a product mix with higher profit margins.

C. The difference between the two companies' ROE in FY15 is very small and Company A's ROE remains similar to Company B's ROE mainly due to Company A increasing its financial leverage.

20. What does the P/E ratio measure?

A. The "multiple" that the stock market places on a company's EPS.

B. The relationship between dividends and market prices.

C. The earnings for one common share of stock.

21. A creditor *most likely* would consider a decrease in which of the following ratios to be positive news?
    A. Interest coverage (times interest earned).
    B. Debt-to-total assets.
    C. Return on assets.

22. When developing forecasts, analysts should *most likely*:
    A. develop possibilities relying exclusively on the results of financial analysis.
    B. use the results of financial analysis, analysis of other information, and judgment.
    C. aim to develop extremely precise forecasts using the results of financial analysis.

CHAPTER 8

⌐RIES

e following:

...es and costs recognized as expenses in the

...cost formulas).

...nd ending inventory using different inven-

...erpetual inventory systems.

...flation of inventory costs on the financial statements and ratios of companies that use different inventory valuation methods (cost formulas or cost flow assumptions).

- Explain LIFO reserve and LIFO liquidation and their effects on financial statements and ratios.
- Convert a company's reported financial statements from LIFO to FIFO for purposes of comparison.
- Describe implications of valuing inventory at net realizable value for financial statements and ratios.
- Describe the financial statement presentation of and disclosures relating to inventories.
- Explain issues that analysts should consider when examining a company's inventory disclosures and other sources of information.
- Analyze and compare the financial statements and ratios of companies, including those that use different inventory valuation methods.

SUMMARY OVERVIEW

- Inventories are a major factor in the analysis of merchandising and manufacturing companies. Such companies generate their sales and profits through inventory transactions on a regular basis. An important consideration in determining profits for these companies is measuring the cost of sales when inventories are sold.

- The total cost of inventories comprises all costs of purchase, costs of conversion, and other costs incurred in bringing the inventories to their present location and condition. Storage costs of finished inventory and abnormal costs due to waste are typically treated as expenses in the period in which they occurred.
- The allowable inventory valuation methods implicitly involve different assumptions about cost flows. The choice of inventory valuation method determines how the cost of goods available for sale during the period is allocated between inventory and cost of sales.
- IFRS allow three inventory valuation methods (cost formulas): first-in, first-out (FIFO); weighted average cost; and specific identification. The specific identification method is used for inventories of items that are not ordinarily interchangeable and for goods or services produced and segregated for specific projects. U.S. GAAP allow these three methods plus the last-in, first-out (LIFO) method. The LIFO method is widely used in the United States for both tax and financial reporting purposes because of potential income tax savings.
- The choice of inventory method affects the financial statements and any financial ratios that are based on them. As a consequence, the analyst must carefully consider inventory valuation method differences when evaluating a company's performance over time or in comparison to industry data or industry competitors.
- A company must use the same cost formula for all inventories having a similar nature and use to the entity.
- The inventory accounting system (perpetual or periodic) may result in different values for cost of sales and ending inventory when the weighted average cost or LIFO inventory valuation method is used.
- Under U.S. GAAP, companies that use the LIFO method must disclose in their financial notes the amount of the LIFO reserve or the amount that would have been reported in inventory if the FIFO method had been used. This information can be used to adjust reported LIFO inventory and cost of goods sold balances to the FIFO method for comparison purposes.
- LIFO liquidation occurs when the number of units in ending inventory declines from the number of units that were present at the beginning of the year. If inventory unit costs have generally risen from year to year, this will produce an inventory-related increase in gross profits.
- Consistency of inventory costing is required under both IFRS and U.S. GAAP. If a company changes an accounting policy, the change must be justifiable and applied retrospectively to the financial statements. An exception to the retrospective restatement is when a company reporting under U.S. GAAP changes to the LIFO method.
- Under IFRS, inventories are measured at the lower of cost and net realizable value. Net realizable value is the estimated selling price in the ordinary course of business less the estimated costs necessary to make the sale. Under U.S. GAAP, inventories are measured at the lower of cost or market value. Market value is defined as current replacement cost subject to an upper limit of net realizable value and a lower limit of net realizable value less a normal profit margin. Reversals of previous write-downs are permissible under IFRS but not under U.S. GAAP.
- Reversals of inventory write-downs may occur under IFRS but are not allowed under U.S. GAAP.
- Changes in the carrying amounts within inventory classifications (such as raw materials, work-in-process, and finished goods) may provide signals about a company's future sales and

profits. Relevant information with respect to inventory management and future sales may be found in the Management Discussion and Analysis or similar items within the annual or quarterly reports, industry news and publications, and industry economic data.

- The inventory turnover ratio, number of days of inventory ratio, and gross profit margin ratio are useful in evaluating the management of a company's inventory.
- Inventory management may have a substantial impact on a company's activity, profitability, liquidity, and solvency ratios. It is critical for the analyst to be aware of industry trends and management's intentions.
- Financial statement disclosures provide information regarding the accounting policies adopted in measuring inventories, the principal uncertainties regarding the use of estimates related to inventories, and details of the inventory carrying amounts and costs. This information can greatly assist analysts in their evaluation of a company's inventory management.

PROBLEMS

1. Inventory cost is *least likely* to include:
   A. production-related storage costs.
   B. costs incurred as a result of normal waste of materials.
   C. transportation costs of shipping inventory to customers.

2. Mustard Seed PLC adheres to IFRS. It recently purchased inventory for €100 million and spent €5 million for storage prior to selling the goods. The amount it charged to inventory expense (€ millions) was *closest* to:
   A. €95.
   B. €100.
   C. €105.

3. Carrying inventory at a value above its historical cost would *most likely* be permitted if:
   A. the inventory was held by a producer of agricultural products.
   B. financial statements were prepared using U.S. GAAP.
   C. the change resulted from a reversal of a previous write-down.

4. Eric's Used Bookstore prepares its financial statements in accordance with IFRS. Inventory was purchased for £1 million and later marked down to £550,000. One of the books, however, was later discovered to be a rare collectible item, and the inventory is now worth an estimated £3 million. The inventory is *most likely* reported on the balance sheet at:
   A. £550,000.
   B. £1,000,000.
   C. £3,000,000.

5. Fernando's Pasta purchased inventory and later wrote it down. The current net realizable value is higher than the value when written down. Fernando's inventory balance will *most likely* be:
   A. higher if it complies with IFRS.
   B. higher if it complies with U.S. GAAP.
   C. the same under U.S. GAAP and IFRS.

For questions 6 through 17, assume the companies use a periodic inventory system.

6. Cinnamon Corp. started business in 2007 and uses the weighted average cost method. During 2007, it purchased 45,000 units of inventory at €10 each and sold 40,000 units for €20 each. In 2008, it purchased another 50,000 units at €11 each and sold 45,000 units for €22 each. Its 2008 cost of sales (€ thousands) was *closest* to:
   A. €490.
   B. €491.
   C. €495.

7. Zimt AG started business in 2007 and uses the FIFO method. During 2007, it purchased 45,000 units of inventory at €10 each and sold 40,000 units for €20 each. In 2008, it purchased another 50,000 units at €11 each and sold 45,000 units for €22 each. Its 2008 ending inventory balance (€ thousands) was *closest* to:
   A. €105.
   B. €109.
   C. €110.

8. Zimt AG uses the FIFO method, and Nutmeg Inc. uses the LIFO method. Compared to the cost of replacing the inventory, during periods of rising prices, the cost of sales reported by:
   A. Zimt is too low.
   B. Nutmeg is too low.
   C. Nutmeg is too high.

9. Zimt AG uses the FIFO method, and Nutmeg Inc. uses the LIFO method. Compared to the cost of replacing the inventory, during periods of rising prices the ending inventory balance reported by:
   A. Zimt is too high.
   B. Nutmeg is too low.
   C. Nutmeg is too high.

10. Like many technology companies, TechnoTools operates in an environment of declining prices. Its reported profits will tend to be *highest* if it accounts for inventory using the:
    A. FIFO method.
    B. LIFO method.
    C. weighted average cost method.

11. Compared to using the weighted average cost method to account for inventory, during a period in which prices are generally rising, the current ratio of a company using the FIFO method would *most likely* be:
    A. lower.
    B. higher.
    C. dependent upon the interaction with accounts payable.

12. Zimt AG wrote down the value of its inventory in 2007 and reversed the write-down in 2008. Compared to the ratios that would have been calculated if the write-down had never occurred, Zimt's reported 2007:
    A. current ratio was too high.
    B. gross margin was too high.
    C. inventory turnover was too high.

13. Zimt AG wrote down the value of its inventory in 2007 and reversed the write-down in 2008. Compared to the results the company would have reported if the write-down had never occurred, Zimt's reported 2008:
    A. profit was overstated.
    B. cash flow from operations was overstated.
    C. year-end inventory balance was overstated.

14. Compared to a company that uses the FIFO method, during periods of rising prices a company that uses the LIFO method will *most likely* appear more:
    A. liquid.
    B. efficient.
    C. profitable.

15. Nutmeg Inc. uses the LIFO method to account for inventory. During years in which inventory unit costs are generally rising and in which the company purchases more inventory than it sells to customers, its reported gross profit margin will *most likely* be:
    A. lower than it would be if the company used the FIFO method.
    B. higher than it would be if the company used the FIFO method.
    C. about the same as it would be if the company used the FIFO method.

16. Compared to using the FIFO method to account for inventory, during periods of rising prices, a company using the LIFO method is *most likely* to report higher:
    A. net income.
    B. cost of sales.
    C. income taxes.

17. Carey Company adheres to U.S. GAAP, whereas Jonathan Company adheres to IFRS. It is *least likely* that:
    A. Carey has reversed an inventory write-down.
    B. Jonathan has reversed an inventory write-down.
    C. Jonathan and Carey both use the FIFO inventory accounting method.

The following information relates to Questions 18 through 25.[1]

Hans Annan, CFA, a food and beverage analyst, is reviewing Century Chocolate's inventory policies as part of his evaluation of the company. Century Chocolate, based in Switzerland, manufactures chocolate products and purchases and resells other confectionery products to complement its chocolate line. Annan visited Century Chocolate's manufacturing facility last year. He learned that cacao beans, imported from Brazil, represent the most significant raw material and that the work-in-progress inventory consists primarily of three items: roasted cacao beans, a thick paste produced from the beans (called chocolate liquor), and a sweetened mixture that needs to be "conched" to produce chocolate. On the tour, Annan learned that the conching process ranges from a few hours for lower-quality products to six days for the highest-quality chocolates. While there, Annan saw the facility's climate-controlled area where manufactured finished products (cocoa and chocolate) and purchased finished goods are stored prior to shipment to customers. After touring the facility, Annan had a discussion with Century Chocolate's CFO regarding the types of costs that were included in each inventory category.

---
[1] Item set developed by Karen Rubsam, CFA (Fountain Hills, Arizona, USA).

Annan has asked his assistant, Joanna Kern, to gather some preliminary information regarding Century Chocolate's financial statements and inventories. He also asked Kern to calculate the inventory turnover ratios for Century Chocolate and another chocolate manufacturer for the most recent five years. Annan does not know Century Chocolate's most direct competitor, so he asks Kern to do some research and select the most appropriate company for the ratio comparison.

Kern reports back that Century Chocolate prepares its financial statements in accordance with IFRS. She tells Annan that the policy footnote states that raw materials and purchased finished goods are valued at purchase cost whereas work in progress and manufactured finished goods are valued at production cost. Raw material inventories and purchased finished goods are accounted for using the FIFO (first-in, first-out) method, and the weighted average cost method is used for other inventories. An allowance is established when the net realizable value of any inventory item is lower than the value calculated.

Kern provides Annan with the selected financial statements and inventory data for Century Chocolate shown in Exhibits A through E. The ratio exhibit Kern prepared compares Century Chocolate's inventory turnover ratios to those of Gordon's Goodies, a U.S.-based company. Annan returns the exhibit and tells Kern to select a different competitor that reports using IFRS rather than U.S. GAAP. During this initial review, Annan asks Kern why she has not indicated whether Century Chocolate uses a perpetual or a periodic inventory system. Kern replies that she learned that Century Chocolate uses a perpetual system but did not include this information in her report because inventory values would be the same under either a perpetual or periodic inventory system. Annan tells Kern she is wrong and directs her to research the matter.

While Kern is revising her analysis, Annan reviews the most recent month's Cocoa Market Review from the International Cocoa Organization. He is drawn to the statement that "the ICCO daily price, averaging prices in both futures markets, reached a 29-year high in US$ terms and a 23-year high in SDRs terms (the SDR unit comprises a basket of major currencies used in international trade: US$, Euro, Pound Sterling, and Yen)." Annan makes a note that he will need to factor the potential continuation of this trend into his analysis.

EXHIBIT A   Century Chocolate Income Statements (CHF millions)

For Years Ended 31 December	2009	2008
Sales	95,290	93,248
Cost of sales	–41,043	–39,047
Marketing, administration, and other expenses	–35,318	–42,481
Profit before taxes	**18,929**	**11,720**
Taxes	–3,283	–2,962
Profit for the period	**15,646**	**8,758**

EXHIBIT B   Century Chocolate Balance Sheets (CHF millions)

For Years Ended 31 December	2009	2008
Cash, cash equivalents, and short-term investments	6,190	8,252
Trade receivables and related accounts, net	11,654	12,910
Inventories, net	8,100	7,039
Other current assets	2,709	2,812
Total current assets	**28,653**	**31,013**

For Years Ended 31 December	2009	2008
Property, plant, and equipment, net	18,291	19,130
Other noncurrent assets	45,144	49,875
Total assets	**92,088**	**100,018**
Trade and other payables	10,931	12,299
Other current liabilities	17,873	25,265
Total current liabilities	**28,804**	**37,564**
Noncurrent liabilities	15,672	14,963
Total liabilities	**44,476**	**52,527**
Equity		
Share capital	332	341
Retained earnings and other reserves	47,280	47,150
Total equity	**47,612**	**47,491**
Total liabilities and shareholders' equity	**92,088**	**100,018**

EXHIBIT C   Century Chocolate Supplementary Footnote Disclosures: Inventories (CHF millions)

For Years Ended 31 December	2009	2008
Raw Materials	2,154	1,585
Work in Progress	1,061	1,027
Finished Goods	5,116	4,665
Total inventories before allowance	8,331	7,277
Allowance for write-downs to net realizable value	−231	−238
Total inventories net of allowance	8,100	7,039

EXHIBIT D   Century Chocolate Inventory Record for Purchased Lemon Drops

Date		Cartons	Per Unit Amount (CHF)
	Beginning inventory	100	22
4 Feb 09	Purchase	40	25
3 Apr 09	Sale	50	32
23 Jul 09	Purchase	70	30
16 Aug 09	Sale	100	32
9 Sep 09	Sale	35	32
15 Nov 09	Purchase	100	28

EXHIBIT E   Century Chocolate Net Realizable Value Information for Black Licorice Jelly Beans

	2009	2008
FIFO cost of inventory at 31 December (CHF)	314,890	374,870
Ending inventory at 31 December (kilograms)	77,750	92,560
Cost per kilogram (CHF)	4.05	4.05
Net realizable value (CHF per kilogram)	4.20	3.95

18. The costs *least likely* to be included by the CFO as inventory are:
    A. storage costs for the chocolate liquor.
    B. excise taxes paid to the government of Brazil for the cacao beans.
    C. storage costs for chocolate and purchased finished goods awaiting shipment to customers.

19. What is the *most likely* justification for Century Chocolate's choice of inventory valuation method for its finished goods?
    A. It is the preferred method under IFRS.
    B. It allocates the same per unit cost to both cost of sales and inventory.
    C. Ending inventory reflects the cost of goods purchased most recently.

20. In Kern's comparative ratio analysis, the 2009 inventory turnover ratio for Century Chocolate is *closest* to:
    A. 5.07.
    B. 5.42.
    C. 5.55.

21. The *most accurate* statement regarding Annan's reasoning for requiring Kern to select a competitor that reports under IFRS for comparative purposes is that under U.S. GAAP:
    A. fair values are used to value inventory.
    B. the LIFO method is permitted to value inventory.
    C. the specific identification method is permitted to value inventory.

22. Annan's statement regarding the perpetual and periodic inventory systems is most significant when which of the following costing systems is used?
    A. LIFO.
    B. FIFO.
    C. Specific identification.

23. Using the inventory record for purchased lemon drops shown in Exhibit D, the cost of sales for 2009 will be *closest* to:
    A. CHF 3,550.
    B. CHF 4,550.
    C. CHF 4,850.

24. Ignoring any tax effect, the 2009 net realizable value reassessment for the black licorice jelly beans will *most likely* result in:
    A. an increase in gross profit of CHF 9,256.
    B. an increase in gross profit of CHF 11,670.
    C. no impact on cost of sales because under IFRS, write-downs cannot be reversed.

25. If the trend noted in the ICCO report continues and Century Chocolate plans to maintain constant or increasing inventory quantities, the *most likely* impact on Century Chocolate's financial statements related to its raw materials inventory will be:
    A. a cost of sales that more closely reflects current replacement values.
    B. a higher allocation of the total cost of goods available for sale to cost of sales.
    C. a higher allocation of the total cost of goods available for sale to ending inventory.

The following information relates to Questions 26 through 31.[2]

John Martinson, CFA, is an equity analyst with a large pension fund. His supervisor, Linda Packard, asks him to write a report on Karp Inc. Karp prepares its financial statements in accordance with U.S. GAAP. Packard is particularly interested in the effects of the company's use of the LIFO method to account for its inventory. For this purpose, Martinson collects the financial data presented in Exhibits F and G.

EXHIBIT F   Balance Sheet Information (US$ millions)

As of 31 December	2009	2008
Cash and cash equivalents	172	157
Accounts receivable	626	458
Inventories	620	539
Other current assets	125	65
Total current assets	1,543	1,219
Property and equipment, net	3,035	2,972
Total assets	4,578	4,191
Total current liabilities	1,495	1,395
Long-term debt	644	604
Total liabilities	2,139	1,999
Common stock and paid in capital	1,652	1,652
Retained earnings	787	540
Total shareholders' equity	2,439	2,192
Total liabilities and shareholders' equity	4,578	4,191

EXHIBIT G   Income Statement Information (US$ millions)

For Years Ended 31 December	2009	2008
Sales	4,346	4,161
Cost of goods sold	2,211	2,147
Depreciation and amortization expense	139	119
Selling, general, and administrative expense	1,656	1,637
Interest expense	31	18
Income tax expense	62	48
Net income	247	192

[2] Item set developed by Rodrigo Ribeiro, CFA (Montevideo, Uruguay).

Martinson finds the following information in the notes to the financial statements:

- The LIFO reserves as of 31 December 2009 and 2008 are $155 million and $117 million, respectively; and
- The effective income tax rate applicable to Karp for 2009 and earlier periods is 20%.

26. If Karp had used FIFO instead of LIFO, the amount of inventory reported as of 31 December 2009 would have been *closest* to:
    A. $465 million.
    B. $658 million.
    C. $775 million.

27. If Karp had used FIFO instead of LIFO, the amount of cost of goods sold reported by Karp for the year ended 31 December 2009 would have been *closest* to:
    A. $2,056 million.
    B. $2,173 million.
    C. $2,249 million.

28. If Karp had used FIFO instead of LIFO, its reported net income for the year ended 31 December 2009 would have been higher by an amount *closest* to:
    A. $30 million.
    B. $38 million.
    C. $155 million.

29. If Karp had used FIFO instead of LIFO, Karp's retained earnings as of 31 December 2009 would have been higher by an amount *closest* to:
    A. $117 million.
    B. $124 million.
    C. $155 million.

30. If Karp had used FIFO instead of LIFO, which of the following ratios computed as of 31 December 2009 would *most likely* have been lower?
    A. cash ratio
    B. current ratio
    C. gross profit margin

31. If Karp had used FIFO instead of LIFO, its debt to equity ratio computed as of 31 December 2009 would have:
    A. increased.
    B. decreased.
    C. remained unchanged.

The following information relates to Questions 32 through 37.[4]

Robert Groff, an equity analyst, is preparing a report on Crux Corp. As part of his report, Groff makes a comparative financial analysis between Crux and its two main competitors, Rolby Corp. and Mikko Inc. Crux and Mikko report under U.S. GAAP and Rolby reports under IFRS.

---

[4] Item set developed by Rodrigo Ribeiro, CFA (Montevideo, Uruguay).

Groff gathers information on Crux, Rolby, and Mikko. The relevant financial information he compiles is in Exhibit H. Some information on the industry is in Exhibit I.

EXHIBIT H   Selected Financial Information (US$ millions)

	Crux	Rolby	Mikko
Inventory valuation method	LIFO	FIFO	LIFO
From the Balance Sheets As of 31 December 2009			
Inventory, gross	480	620	510
Valuation allowance	20	25	14
Inventory, net	460	595	496
Total debt	1,122	850	732
Total shareholders' equity	2,543	2,403	2,091
As of 31 December 2008			
Inventory, gross	465	602	401
Valuation allowance	23	15	12
Inventory, net	442	587	389
From the Income Statements Year Ended 31 December 2009			
Revenues	4,609	5,442	3,503
Cost of goods sold[a]	3,120	3,782	2,550
Net income	229	327	205
	13	15	15
LIFO Reserve			
As of 31 December 2009	55	0	77
As of 31 December 2008	72	0	50
As of 31 December 2007	96	0	43
Tax Rate			
Effective tax rate	30%	30%	30%

[a]Charges included in cost of goods sold for inventory write-downs. (This does not match the change in the inventory valuation allowance because the valuation allowance is reduced to reflect the valuation allowance attached to items sold and increased for additional necessary write-downs.)

EXHIBIT I   Industry Information

	2009	2008	2007
Raw materials price index	112	105	100
Finished goods price index	114	106	100

To compare the financial performance of the three companies, Groff decides to convert LIFO figures into FIFO figures, and adjust figures to assume no valuation allowance is recognized by any company.

After reading Groff's draft report, his supervisor, Rachel Borghi, asks him the following questions:

Question 1: Which company's gross profit margin would best reflect current costs of the industry?

Question 2: Would Rolby's valuation method show a higher gross profit margin than Crux's under an inflationary, a deflationary, or a stable price scenario?

Question 3: Which group of ratios usually appears more favorable with an inventory write-down?

32. Crux's inventory turnover ratio computed as of 31 December 2009, after the adjustments suggested by Groff, is *closest* to:
    A. 5.67.
    B. 5.83.
    C. 6.13.

33. Rolby's net profit margin for the year ended 31 December 2009, after the adjustments suggested by Groff, is *closest* to:
    A. 6.01%.
    B. 6.20%.
    C. 6.28%.

34. Compared with its unadjusted debt-to-equity ratio, Mikko's debt-to-equity ratio as of 31 December 2009, after the adjustments suggested by Groff, is:
    A. lower.
    B. higher.
    C. the same.

35. The *best* answer to Borghi's Question 1 is:
    A. Crux's.
    B. Rolby's.
    C. Mikko's.

36. The *best* answer to Borghi's Question 2 is:
    A. stable.
    B. inflationary.
    C. deflationary.

37. The *best* answer to Borghi's Question 3 is:
    A. Activity ratios.
    B. Solvency ratios.
    C. Profitability ratios.

The following information relates to Questions 38 through 45.[23]

ZP Corporation is a (hypothetical) multinational corporation headquartered in Japan that trades on numerous stock exchanges. ZP prepares its consolidated financial statements

---

[23] Item set developed by Karen O'Connor Rubsam, CFA (Fountain Hills, Arizona, U.S.A.).

in accordance with U.S. GAAP. Excerpts from ZP's 2009 annual report are shown in Exhibits J–L.

EXHIBIT J   Consolidated Balance Sheets (¥ millions)

Year Ended 31 December	2008	2009
Current assets		
Cash and cash equivalents	¥542,849	¥814,760
⋮	⋮	⋮
Inventories	608,572	486,465
⋮	⋮	⋮
Total current assets	4,028,742	3,766,309
⋮	⋮	⋮
Total assets	**¥10,819,440**	**¥9,687,346**
⋮	⋮	⋮
Total current liabilities	¥3,980,247	¥3,529,765
⋮	⋮	⋮
Total long-term liabilities	2,663,795	2,624,002
Minority interest in consolidated subsidiaries	218,889	179,843
Total shareholders' equity	3,956,509	3,353,736
Total liabilities and shareholders' equity	**¥10,819,440**	**¥9,687,346**

EXHIBIT K   Consolidated Statements of Income (¥ millions)

For the years ended 31 December	2007	2008	2009
Net revenues			
Sales of products	¥7,556,699	¥8,273,503	¥6,391,240
Financing operations	425,998	489,577	451,950
	7,982,697	8,763,080	6,843,190
Cost and expenses			
Cost of products sold	6,118,742	6,817,446	5,822,805
Cost of financing operations	290,713	356,005	329,128
Selling, general and administrative	827,005	832,837	844,927
⋮	⋮	⋮	⋮
Operating income (loss)	746,237	756,792	– 153,670
⋮	⋮	⋮	⋮
Net income	**¥548,011**	**¥572,626**	**¥–145,646**

EXHIBIT L   Selected Disclosures in the 2009 Annual Report

Management's Discussion and Analysis of Financial Condition and Results of Operations
"Cost reduction efforts were offset by increased prices of raw materials, other production materials and parts." . . . "Inventories decreased during fiscal 2009 by ¥122.1 billion, or 20.1%, to ¥486.5 billion. This reflects the impacts of decreased sales volumes and fluctuations in foreign currency translation rates."

Management and Corporate Information
Risk Factors
Industry and Business Risks
The worldwide market for our products is highly competitive. ZP faces intense competition from other manufacturers in the respective markets in which it operates. Competition has intensified due to the worldwide deterioration in economic conditions. In addition, competition is likely to further intensify because of continuing globalization, possibly resulting in industry reorganization. Factors affecting competition include product quality and features, the amount of time required for innovation and development, pricing, reliability, safety, economy in use, customer service, and financing terms. Increased competition may lead to lower unit sales and excess production capacity and excess inventory. This may result in a further downward price pressure.

ZP's ability to adequately respond to the recent rapid changes in the industry and to maintain its competitiveness will be fundamental to its future success in maintaining and expanding its market share in existing and new markets.

Notes to Consolidated Financial Statements
2. Summary of significant accounting policies:
Inventories. Inventories are valued at cost, not in excess of market. Cost is determined on the "average-cost" basis, except for the cost of finished products carried by certain subsidiary companies which is determined "last-in, first-out" ("LIFO") basis. Inventories valued on the LIFO basis totaled ¥94,578 million and ¥50,037 million at 31 December 2008 and 2009, respectively. Had the "first-in, first-out" basis been used for those companies using the LIFO basis, inventories would have been ¥10,120 million and ¥19,660 million higher than reported at 31 December 2008 and 2009, respectively.

9. Inventories:
Inventories consist of the following:

Year Ended 31 December (Yen in millions)	2008	2009
Finished goods	¥403,856	¥291,977
Raw materials	99,869	85,966
Work in process	79,979	83,890
Supplies and other	24,868	24,632
	¥608,572	**¥486,465**

38. The MD&A indicated that the prices of raw material, other production materials, and parts increased. Based on the inventory valuation methods described in Note 2, which inventory classification would *least* accurately reflect current prices?

    A. Raw materials

    B. Finished goods

    C. Work in process

39. The 2008 inventory value as reported on the 2009 consolidated balance sheet if the company had used the FIFO inventory valuation method instead of the LIFO inventory valuation method for a portion of its inventory would be *closest* to:

    A. ¥104,698 million.

    B. ¥506,125 million.

    C. ¥618,692 million.

40. What is the *least likely* reason why ZP may need to change its accounting policies regarding inventory at some point after 2009?

    A. The U.S. SEC is likely to require companies to use the same inventory valuation method for all inventories.

    B. The U.S. SEC is likely to prohibit the use of one of the methods ZP currently uses for inventory valuation.

    C. One of the inventory valuation methods used for U.S. tax purposes may be repealed as an acceptable method.

41. If ZP had prepared its financial statement in accordance with IFRS, the inventory turnover ratio (using average inventory) for 2009 would be:

    A. lower.

    B. higher.

    C. the same.

42. Inventory levels decreased from 2008 to 2009 for all of the following reasons *except*:

    A. LIFO liquidation.

    B. sales volume decreased.

    C. fluctuations in foreign currency translation rates.

43. Which observation is *most likely* a result of looking only at the information reported in Note 9?

    A. Increased competition has led to lower unit sales.

    B. There have been significant price increases in supplies.

    C. Management expects a further downturn in sales during 2010.

44. Note 2 indicates that, "Inventories valued on the LIFO basis totaled ¥94,578 million and ¥50,037 million at 31 December 2008 and 2009, respectively." Based on this, the LIFO reserve should *most likely*:

    A. increase.

    B. decrease.

    C. remain the same.

45. The Industry and Business Risk excerpt states that, "Increased competition may lead to lower unit sales and excess production capacity and excess inventory. This may result in a further downward price pressure." The downward price pressure could lead to inventory that is valued above current market prices or net realizable value. Any write-downs of inventory are *least likely* to have a significant effect on the inventory valued using:

    A. weighted average cost.

    B. first-in, first-out (FIFO).

    C. last-in, first-out (LIFO).

CHAPTER 9

LONG-LIVED ASSETS

LEARNING OUTCOMES

After completing this chapter, you will be able to do the following:

- Distinguish between costs that are capitalized and costs that are expensed in the period in which they are incurred.
- Compare the financial reporting of the following classifications of intangible assets: purchased, internally developed, acquired in a business combination.
- Explain and evaluate the effects on financial statements and ratios of capitalizing versus expensing costs in the period in which they are incurred.
- Describe the different depreciation methods for property, plant, and equipment and the effects of the choice of depreciation method and the assumptions concerning useful life and residual value on depreciation expense, financial statements, and ratios.
- Calculate depreciation expense.
- Describe the different amortization methods for intangible assets with finite lives and the effects of the choice of amortization method and the assumptions concerning useful life and residual value on amortization expense, financial statements, and ratios.
- Calculate amortization expense.
- Describe the revaluation model.
- Describe the impairment of property, plant, and equipment and intangible assets.
- Describe the derecognition of property, plant, and equipment and intangible assets.
- Explain and evaluate the effects on financial statements and ratios of impairment, revaluation, and derecognition of property, plant, and equipment and intangible assets.
- Describe the financial statement presentation of and disclosures relating to property, plant, and equipment and intangible assets.
- Analyze and interpret the financial statement disclosures regarding property, plant, and equipment and intangible assets.
- Compare the financial reporting of investment property with that of property, plant, and equipment.

- Explain and evaluate the effects on financial statements and ratios of leasing assets instead of purchasing them.
- Explain and evaluate the effects on financial statements and ratios of finance leases and operating leases from the perspectives of both the lessor and the lessee.

SUMMARY OVERVIEW

- Expenditures related to long-lived assets are capitalized as part of the cost of assets if they are expected to provide future benefits, typically beyond one year. Otherwise, expenditures related to long-lived assets are expensed as incurred.
- Although capitalizing expenditures, rather than expensing them, results in higher reported profitability in the initial year, it results in lower profitability in subsequent years; however, if a company continues to purchase similar or increasing amounts of assets each year, the profitability-enhancing effect of capitalization continues.
- Capitalizing an expenditure rather than expensing it results in a greater amount reported as cash from operations because capitalized expenditures are classified as an investing cash outflow rather than an operating cash outflow.
- Companies must capitalize interest costs associated with acquiring or constructing an asset that requires a long period of time to prepare for its intended use.
- Including capitalized interest in the calculation of interest coverage ratios provides a better assessment of a company's solvency.
- IFRS require research costs be expensed but allow all development costs (not only software development costs) to be capitalized under certain conditions. Generally, U.S. accounting standards require that research and development costs be expensed; however, certain costs related to software development are required to be capitalized.
- When one company acquires another company, the transaction is accounted for using the acquisition method of accounting in which the company identified as the acquirer allocates the purchase price to each asset acquired (and each liability assumed) on the basis of its fair value. Under acquisition accounting, if the purchase price of an acquisition exceeds the sum of the amounts that can be allocated to individual identifiable assets and liabilities, the excess is recorded as goodwill.
- The capitalized costs of long-lived tangible assets and of intangible assets with finite useful lives are allocated to expense in subsequent periods over their useful lives. For tangible assets, this process is referred to as depreciation, and for intangible assets, it is referred to as amortization.
- Long-lived tangible assets and intangible assets with finite useful lives are reviewed for impairment whenever changes in events or circumstances indicate that the carrying amount of an asset may not be recoverable.
- Intangible assets with an indefinite useful life are not amortized but are reviewed for impairment annually.
- Impairment disclosures can provide useful information about a company's expected cash flows.
- Methods of calculating depreciation or amortization expense include the straight-line method, in which the cost of an asset is allocated to expense in equal amounts each year over its useful life; accelerated methods, in which the allocation of cost is greater in earlier years; and

the units-of-production method, in which the allocation of cost corresponds to the actual use of an asset in a particular period.

- Estimates required for depreciation and amortization calculations include the useful life of the equipment (or its total lifetime productive capacity) and its expected residual value at the end of that useful life. A longer useful life and higher expected residual value result in a smaller amount of annual depreciation relative to a shorter useful life and lower expected residual value.
- IFRS permit the use of either the cost model or the revaluation model for the valuation and reporting of long-lived assets, but the revaluation model is not allowed under U.S. GAAP.
- Under the revaluation model, carrying amounts are the fair values at the date of revaluation less any subsequent accumulated depreciation or amortization.
- In contrast with depreciation and amortization charges, which serve to allocate the cost of a long-lived asset over its useful life, impairment charges reflect an unexpected decline in the fair value of an asset to an amount lower than its carrying amount.
- IFRS permit impairment losses to be reversed, with the reversal reported in profit. U.S. GAAP do not permit the reversal of impairment losses.
- The gain or loss on the sale of long-lived assets is computed as the sales proceeds minus the carrying amount of the asset at the time of sale.
- Estimates of average age and remaining useful life of a company's assets reflect the relationship between assets accounted for on a historical cost basis and depreciation amounts.
- The average remaining useful life of a company's assets can be estimated as net PPE divided by depreciation expense, although the accounting useful life may not necessarily correspond to the economic useful life.
- Long-lived assets reclassified as held for sale cease to be depreciated or amortized. Long-lived assets to be disposed of other than by a sale (e.g., by abandonment, exchange for another asset, or distribution to owners in a spin-off) are classified as held for use until disposal. Thus, they continue to be depreciated and tested for impairment.
- Investment property is defined as property that is owned (or, in some cases, leased under a finance lease) for the purpose of earning rentals, capital appreciation, or both.
- Under IFRS, companies are allowed to value investment properties using either a cost model or a fair value model. The cost model is identical to the cost model used for property, plant, and equipment, but the fair value model differs from the revaluation model used for property, plant, and equipment. Under the fair value model, all changes in the fair value of investment property affect net income.
- Under U.S. GAAP, investment properties are generally measured using the cost model.
- Accounting standards generally define two types of leases: operating leases and finance (or capital) leases. Current U.S. GAAP specify four criteria to determine when a lease is classified as a capital lease, although proposed standards would eliminate those specific criteria. IFRS are less prescriptive in determining the classification of a lease as a finance lease.
- When a lessee reports a lease as an operating lease rather than a finance lease, it usually appears more profitable in early years of the lease and less so later, and it appears less leveraged over the entire lease period.
- When a lessor reports a lease as a finance lease rather than an operating lease, it usually appears more profitable in early years of the lease.

PROBLEMS

1. JOOVI Inc. has recently purchased and installed a new machine for its manufacturing plant. The company incurred the following costs:

Purchase price	$12,980
Freight and insurance	$1,200
Installation	$700
Testing	$100
Maintenance staff training costs	$500

The total cost of the machine to be shown on JOOVI's balance sheet is *closest* to:
A. $14,180.
B. $14,980.
C. $15,480.

2. BAURU, S.A., a Brazilian corporation, borrows capital from a local bank to finance the construction of its manufacturing plant. The loan has the following conditions:

Borrowing date	1 January 2009
Amount borrowed	500 million Brazilian real (BRL)
Annual interest rate	14 percent
Term of the loan	3 years
Payment method	Annual payment of interest only. Principal amortization is due at the end of the loan term.

The construction of the plant takes two years, during which time BAURU earned BRL 10 million by temporarily investing the loan proceeds. Which of the following is the amount of interest related to the plant construction (in BRL million) that can be capitalized in BAURU's balance sheet?
A. 130
B. 140
C. 210

3. After reading the financial statements and footnotes of a company that follows IFRS, an analyst identified the following intangible assets:
   • product patent expiring in 40 years
   • copyright with no expiration date
   • goodwill acquired 2 years ago in a business combination

Which of these assets is an intangible asset with a finite useful life?

	Product Patent	Copyright	Goodwill
A.	Yes	Yes	No
B.	Yes	No	No
C.	No	Yes	Yes

4. Intangible assets with finite useful lives *mostly* differ from intangible assets with infinite useful lives with respect to accounting treatment of:
   A. revaluation.
   B. impairment.
   C. amortization.

5. A financial analyst is studying the income statement effect of two alternative depreciation methods for a recently acquired piece of equipment. She gathers the following information about the equipment's expected production life and use:

	Year 1	Year 2	Year 3	Year 4	Year 5	Total
Units of production	2,000	2,000	2,000	2,000	2,500	10,500

   Compared with the units-of-production method of depreciation, if the company uses the straight-line method to depreciate the equipment, its net income in Year 1 will *most likely* be:
   A. lower.
   B. higher.
   C. the same.

6. Juan Martinez, CFO of VIRMIN, S.A., is selecting the depreciation method to use for a new machine. The machine has an expected useful life of six years. Production is expected to be relatively low initially but to increase over time. The method chosen for tax reporting must be the same as the method used for financial reporting. If Martinez wants to minimize tax payments in the first year of the machine's life, which of the following depreciation methods is Martinez *most likely* to use?
   A. Straight-line method
   B. Units-of-production method
   C. Double-declining balance method

The following information relates to Questions 7 and 8.

Miguel Rodriguez of MARIO, S.A., an Uruguayan corporation, is computing the depreciation expense of a piece of manufacturing equipment for the fiscal year ended 31 December 2009. The equipment was acquired on 1 January 2009. Rodriguez gathers the following information (currency in Uruguayan pesos, UYP):

Cost of the equipment	UYP 1,200,000
Estimated residual value	UYP 200,000
Expected useful life	8 years
Total productive capacity	800,000 units
Production in FY 2009	135,000 units
Expected production for the next 7 years	95,000 units each year

7. If MARIO uses the straight-line method, the amount of depreciation expense on MARIO's income statement related to the manufacturing equipment is *closest* to:
   A. 125,000.
   B. 150,000.
   C. 168,750.

8. If MARIO uses the units-of-production method, the amount of depreciation expense (in UYP) on MARIO's income statement related to the manufacturing equipment is *closest* to:
   A. 118,750.
   B. 168,750.
   C. 202,500.

9. Which of the following amortization methods is *most likely* to evenly distribute the cost of an intangible asset over its useful life?
   A. Straight-line method
   B. Units-of-production method
   C. Double-declining balance method

10. Which of the following will cause a company to show a lower amount of amortization of intangible assets in the first year after acquisition?
    A. A higher residual value
    B. A higher amortization rate
    C. A shorter useful life

11. An analyst in the finance department of BOOLDO, S.A., a French corporation, is computing the amortization of a customer list, an intangible asset, for the fiscal year ended 31 December 2009. She gathers the following information about the asset:

Acquisition cost	€2,300,000
Acquisition date	1 January 2008
Expected residual value at time of acquisition	€500,000
The customer list is expected to result in extra sales for three years after acquisition. The present value of these expected extra sales exceeds the cost of the list.	

If the analyst uses the straight-line method, the amount of accumulated amortization related to the customer list as of 31 December 2009 is *closest* to:
   A. €600,000.
   B. €1,200,000.
   C. €1,533,333.

12. A financial analyst is analyzing the amortization of a product patent acquired by MAKETTI S.p.A., an Italian corporation. He gathers the following information about the patent:

Acquisition cost	€5,800,000
Acquisition date	1 January 2009
Patent expiration date	31 December 2015
Total plant capacity of patented product	40,000 units per year
Production of patented product in fiscal year ended 31 December 2009	20,000 units
Expected production of patented product during life of the patent	175,000 units

If the analyst uses the units-of-production method, the amortization expense on the patent for fiscal year 2009 is *closest* to:
   A. €414,286.
   B. €662,857.
   C. €828,571.

13. MARU S.A. de C.V., a Mexican corporation that follows IFRS, has elected to use the revaluation model for its property, plant, and equipment. One of MARU's machines was purchased for 2,500,000 Mexican pesos (MXN) at the beginning of the fiscal year ended 31 March 2010. As of 31 March 2010, the machine has a fair value of MXN 3,000,000. Should MARU show a profit for the revaluation of the machine?
    A. Yes.
    B. No, because this revaluation is recorded directly in equity.
    C. No, because value increases resulting from revaluation can never be recognized as a profit.

14. An analyst is studying the impairment of the manufacturing equipment of WLP Corp., a U.K.-based corporation that follows IFRS. He gathers the following information about the equipment:

Fair value	£16,800,000
Costs to sell	£800,000
Value in use	£14,500,000
Net carrying amount	£19,100,000

   The amount of the impairment loss on WLP Corp.'s income statement related to its manufacturing equipment is *closest* to:
    A. £2,300,000.
    B. £3,100,000.
    C. £4,600,000.

15. A financial analyst at BETTO, S.A. is analyzing the result of the sale of a vehicle for 85,000 Argentine pesos (ARP) on 31 December 2009. The analyst compiles the following information about the vehicle:

Acquisition cost of the vehicle	ARP 100,000
Acquisition date	1 January 2007
Estimated residual value at acquisition date	ARP 10,000
Expected useful life	9 years
Depreciation method	Straight-line

   The result of the sale of the vehicle is *most likely*:
    A. a loss of ARP 15,000.
    B. a gain of ARP 15,000.
    C. a gain of ARP 18,333.

16. CROCO S.p.A. sells an intangible asset with a historical acquisition cost of €12 million and an accumulated depreciation of €2 million and reports a loss on the sale of €3.2 million. Which of the following amounts is *most likely* the sale price of the asset?
    A. €6.8 million
    B. €8.8 million
    C. €13.2 million

17. According to IFRS, all of the following pieces of information about property, plant, and equipment must be disclosed in a company's financial statements and footnotes *except for*:
    A. useful lives.
    B. acquisition dates.
    C. amount of disposals.

18. According to IFRS, all of the following pieces of information about intangible assets must be disclosed in a company's financial statements and footnotes *except for*:
    A. fair value.
    B. impairment loss.
    C. amortization rate.

19. Which of the following characteristics is *most likely* to differentiate investment property from property, plant, and equipment?
    A. It is tangible.
    B. It earns rent.
    C. It is long-lived.

20. If a company uses the fair value model to value investment property, changes in the fair value of the asset are *least likely* to affect:
    A. net income.
    B. net operating income.
    C. other comprehensive income.

21. Investment property is *most likely* to:
    A. earn rent.
    B. be held for resale.
    C. be used in the production of goods and services.

22. A company is *most likely* to:
    A. use a fair value model for some investment property and a cost model for other investment property.
    B. change from the fair value model when transactions on comparable properties become less frequent.
    C. change from the fair value model when the company transfers investment property to property, plant, and equipment.

The following information relates to Questions 23 through 28.[1]

Melanie Hart, CFA, is a transportation analyst. Hart has been asked to write a research report on Altai Mountain Rail Company (AMRC). Like other companies in the railroad industry, AMRC's operations are capital intensive, with significant investments in such long-lived tangible assets as property, plant, and equipment. In November of 2008, AMRC's board of directors hired a new team to manage the company. In reviewing the company's 2009 annual report, Hart is concerned about some of the accounting choices that the new management has made. These choices differ from those of the previous management and from common industry practice. Hart has highlighted the following statements from the company's annual report:

---

[1] Item set developed by Christopher Anderson, CFA (Lawrence, Kansas, U.S.A.)

Statement 1:	"In 2009, AMRC spent significant amounts on track replacement and similar improvements. AMRC expensed rather than capitalized a significant proportion of these expenditures."
Statement 2:	"AMRC uses the straight-line method of depreciation for both financial and tax reporting purposes to account for plant and equipment."
Statement 3:	"In 2009, AMRC recognized an impairment loss of €50 million on a fleet of locomotives. The impairment loss was reported as 'other income' in the income statement and reduced the carrying amount of the assets on the balance sheet."
Statement 4:	"AMRC acquires the use of many of its assets, including a large portion of its fleet of rail cars, under long-term lease contracts. In 2009, AMRC acquired the use of equipment with a fair value of €200 million under 20-year lease contracts. These leases were classified as operating leases. Prior to 2009, most of these lease contracts were classified as finance leases."

Exhibits A and B contain AMRC's 2009 consolidated income statement and balance sheet. AMRC prepares its financial statements in accordance with International Financial Reporting Standards.

EXHIBIT A   Consolidated Statement of Income

	2009		2008	
For the years ended 31 December	€ in millions	% Revenues	€ in millions	% Revenues
Operating revenues	2,600	100.0%	2,300	100.0%
Operating expenses				
Depreciation	(200)	(7.7%)	(190)	(8.3%)
Lease payments	(210)	(8.1%)	(195)	(8.5%)
Other operating expense	(1,590)	(61.1%)	(1,515)	(65.9%)
Total operating expenses	(2,000)	(76.9%)	(1,900)	(82.6%)
Operating income	600	23.1%	400	17.4%
Other income	(50)	(1.9%)	—	0.0%
Interest expense	(73)	(2.8%)	(69)	(3.0%)
Income before taxes	477	18.4%	331	14.4%
Income taxes	(189)	(7.3%)	(125)	(5.4%)
Net income	288	11.1%	206	9.0%

EXHIBIT B   Consolidated Balance Sheet

	2009		2008	
As of 31 December	€ in millions	% Assets	€ in millions	% Assets
Assets				
Current assets	500	9.4%	450	8.5%
Property & equipment:				
Land	700	13.1%	700	13.2%
Plant & equipment	6,000	112.1%	5,800	109.4%
Total property & equipment	6,700	125.2%	6,500	122.6%

(continued)

EXHIBIT B   (Continued)

As of 31 December	2009		2008	
	€ in millions	% Assets	€ in millions	% Assets
Accumulated depreciation	(1,850)	(34.6%)	(1,650)	(31.1%)
Net property & equipment	4,850	90.6%	4,850	91.5%
Total assets	5,350	100.0%	5,300	100.0%
Liabilities and Shareholders' Equity				
Current liabilities	480	9.0%	430	8.1%
Long-term debt	1,030	19.3%	1,080	20.4%
Other long-term provisions and liabilities	1,240	23.1%	1,440	27.2%
Total liabilities	2,750	51.4%	2,950	55.7%
Shareholders' equity				
Common stock and paid-in-surplus	760	14.2%	760	14.3%
Retained earnings	1,888	35.3%	1,600	30.2%
Other comprehensive losses	(48)	(0.9%)	(10)	(0.2%)
Total shareholders' equity	2,600	48.6%	2,350	44.3%
Total liabilities & shareholders' equity	5,350	100.0%	5,300	100.0%

23. With respect to Statement 1, which of the following is the *most likely* effect of management's decision to expense rather than capitalize these expenditures?
    A. 2009 net profit margin is higher than if the expenditures had been capitalized.
    B. 2009 total asset turnover is lower than if the expenditures had been capitalized.
    C. Future profit growth will be higher than if the expenditures had been capitalized.

24. With respect to Statement 2, what would be the *most likely* effect in 2010 if AMRC were to switch to an accelerated depreciation method for both financial and tax reporting?
    A. Net profit margin would decrease.
    B. Total asset turnover would increase.
    C. Cash flow from operating activities would increase.

25. With respect to Statement 3, what is the *most likely* effect of the impairment loss?
    A. Net income in years prior to 2009 was likely understated.
    B. Net profit margins in years after 2009 will likely exceed the 2009 net profit margin.
    C. Cash flow from operating activities in 2009 was likely lower due to the impairment loss.

26. Based on Exhibits A and B, the *best estimate* of the average remaining useful life of the company's plant and equipment at the end of 2009 is:
    A. 20.75 years.
    B. 24.25 years.
    C. 30.00 years.

27. With respect to Statement 4, if AMRC had used its old classification method for its leases instead of its new classification method, its 2009 total asset turnover ratio would *most likely* be:
    A. lower.
    B. higher.
    C. the same.

28. With respect to Statement 4 and Exhibit A, if AMRC had used its old classification method for its leases instead of its new classification method, the *most likely* effect on its 2009 ratios would be a:
    A. higher net profit margin.
    B. higher fixed asset turnover.
    C. higher total liabilities-to-total assets ratio.

The following information relates to Questions 29 through 35.[2]

Brian Jordan is interviewing for a junior equity analyst position at Orion Investment Advisors. As part of the interview process, Mary Benn, Orion's Director of Research, provides Jordan with information about two hypothetical companies, Alpha and Beta, and asks him to comment on the information on their financial statements and ratios. Both companies prepare their financial statements in accordance with International Financial Reporting Standards (IFRS) and are identical in all respects except for their accounting choices.

Jordan is told that at the beginning of the current fiscal year, both companies purchased a major new computer system and began building new manufacturing plants for their own use. Alpha capitalized and Beta expensed the cost of the computer system; Alpha capitalized and Beta expensed the interest costs associated with the construction of the manufacturing plants. In mid-year, both companies leased new office headquarters. Alpha classified the lease as an operating lease, and Beta classified it as a finance lease.

Benn asks Jordan, "What was the impact of these decisions on each company's current fiscal year financial statements and ratios?"

Jordan responds, "Alpha's decision to capitalize the cost of its new computer system instead of expensing it results in lower net income, lower total assets, and higher cash flow from operating activities in the current fiscal year. Alpha's decision to capitalize its interest costs instead of expensing them results in a lower fixed asset turnover ratio and a higher interest coverage ratio. Alpha's decision to classify its lease as an operating lease instead of a finance lease results in higher net income, higher cash flow from operating activities, and stronger solvency and activity ratios compared to Beta."

Jordan is told that Alpha uses the straight-line depreciation method and Beta uses an accelerated depreciation method; both companies estimate the same useful lives for long-lived assets. Many companies in their industry use the units-of-production method.

Benn asks Jordan, "What are the financial statement implications of each depreciation method, and how do you determine a company's need to reinvest in its productive capacity?"

Jordan replies, "All other things being equal, the straight-line depreciation method results in the least variability of net profit margin over time, while an accelerated depreciation method results in a declining trend in net profit margin over time. The units-of-production can result in a net profit margin trend that is quite variable. I use a three-step approach to estimate a company's need to reinvest in its productive capacity. First, I estimate the average age of the assets by dividing net property, plant, and equipment by annual depreciation expense. Second, I estimate the average remaining useful life of the assets by dividing accumulated depreciation by depreciation expense. Third, I add the estimates of the average remaining useful life and the average age of the assets in order to determine the total useful life."

Jordan is told that at the end of the current fiscal year, Alpha revalued a manufacturing plant; this increased its reported carrying amount by 15 percent. There was no previous downward revaluation of the plant. Beta recorded an impairment loss on a manufacturing plant; this reduced its carrying by 10 percent.

---

[2] Item set developed by Philip Fanara Jr., CFA (Hyattsville, Maryland, U.S.A)

Benn asks Jordan "What was the impact of these decisions on each company's current fiscal year financial ratios?"

Jordan responds, "Beta's impairment loss increases its debt to total assets and fixed asset turnover ratios, and lowers its cash flow from operating activities. Alpha's revaluation increases its debt to capital and return on assets ratios, and reduces its return on equity."

At the end of the interview, Benn thanks Jordan for his time and states that a hiring decision will be made shortly.

29. Jordan's response about the financial statement impact of Alpha's decision to capitalize the cost of its new computer system is most likely *correct* with respect to:
   A. lower net income.
   B. lower total assets.
   C. higher cash flow from operating activities.

30. Jordan's response about the ratio impact of Alpha's decision to capitalize interest costs is most likely *correct* with respect to the:
   A. interest coverage ratio.
   B. fixed asset turnover ratio.
   C. interest coverage and fixed asset turnover ratios.

31. Jordan's response about the impact of Alpha's decision to classify its lease as an operating lease instead of finance lease is most likely *incorrect* with respect to:
   A. net income.
   B. solvency and activity ratios.
   C. cash flow from operating activities.

32. Jordan's response about the impact of the different depreciation methods on net profit margin is most likely *incorrect* with respect to:
   A. accelerated depreciation.
   B. straight-line depreciation.
   C. units-of-production depreciation.

33. Jordan's response about his approach to estimating a company's need to reinvest in its productive capacity is most likely *correct* regarding:
   A. estimating the average age of the asset base.
   B. estimating the total useful life of the asset base.
   C. estimating the average remaining useful life of the asset base.

34. Jordan's response about the effect of Beta's impairment loss is most likely *incorrect* with respect to the impact on its:
   A. debt to total assets.
   B. fixed asset turnover.
   C. cash flow from operating activities.

35. Jordan's response about the effect of Alpha's revaluation is most likely *correct* with respect to the impact on its:
   A. return on equity.
   B. return on assets.
   C. debt to capital ratio.

CHAPTER **10**

NON-CURRENT (LONG-TERM) LIABILITIES

LEARNING OUTCOMES

After completing this chapter, you will be able to do the following:

- determine the initial recognition, initial measurement, and subsequent measurement of bonds;
- describe the effective interest method and calculate interest expense, amortisation of bond discounts/premiums, and interest payments;
- explain the derecognition of debt;
- describe the role of debt covenants in protecting creditors;
- describe the financial statement presentation of and disclosures relating to debt;
- explain motivations for leasing assets instead of purchasing them;
- distinguish between a finance lease and an operating lease from the perspectives of the lessor and the lessee;
- determine the initial recognition, initial measurement, and subsequent measurement of finance leases;
- compare the disclosures relating to finance and operating leases;
- compare the presentation and disclosure of defined contribution and defined benefit pension plans;
- calculate and interpret leverage and coverage ratios.

SUMMARY OVERVIEW

- The sales proceeds of a bond issue are determined by discounting future cash payments using the market rate of interest at the time of issuance (effective interest rate). The reported interest expense on bonds is based on the effective interest rate.

- Future cash payments on bonds usually include periodic interest payments (made at the stated interest rate or coupon rate) and the principal amount at maturity.
- When the market rate of interest equals the coupon rate for the bonds, the bonds will sell at par (i.e., at a price equal to the face value). When the market rate of interest is higher than the bonds' coupon rate, the bonds will sell at a discount. When the market rate of interest is lower than the bonds' coupon rate, the bonds will sell at a premium.
- An issuer amortises any issuance discount or premium on bonds over the life of the bonds.
- If a company redeems bonds before maturity, it reports a gain or loss on debt extinguishment computed as the net carrying amount of the bonds (including bond issuance costs under IFRS) less the amount required to redeem the bonds.
- Debt covenants impose restrictions on borrowers, such as limitations on future borrowing or requirements to maintain a minimum debt-to-equity ratio.
- The carrying amount of bonds is typically amortised historical cost, which can differ from their fair value.
- Companies are required to disclose the fair value of financial liabilities, including debt. Although permitted to do so, few companies opt to report debt at fair values on the balance sheet.
- Accounting standards require leases to be classified as either operating leases or finance (capital) leases. Leases are classified as finance leases when substantially all the risks and rewards of legal ownership are transferred to the lessee.
- When a lessee reports a lease as an operating lease rather than a finance lease, the lessee usually appears more profitable in the early years of the lease and less so later, and it appears more solvent over the whole period.
- When a lessor reports a lease as a finance lease rather than an operating lease, the lessor usually appears more profitable in the early years of the lease.
- In a finance lease where the present value of lease payments equals the carrying amount of the leased asset, a lessor earns only interest revenue. In a finance lease where the present value of lease payments exceeds the carrying amount of the leased asset, a lessor earns both interest revenue and a profit (or loss) on the sale of the leased asset.
- Two types of pension plans are defined contribution plans and defined benefits plans. In a defined contribution plan, the amount of contribution into the plan is specified (i.e., defined) and the amount of pension that is ultimately paid by the plan (received by the retiree) depends on the performance of the plan's assets. In a defined benefit plan, the amount of pension that is ultimately paid by the plan (received by the retiree) is defined, usually according to a benefit formula.
- Under a defined contribution plan, the cash payment made into the plan is recognised as pension expense.
- Under both IFRS and US GAAP, companies must report the difference between the defined benefit pension obligation and the pension assets as an asset or liability on the balance sheet.
- Under IFRS, the change in the defined benefit plan net asset or liability is recognised as a cost of the period, with two components of the change (service cost and net interest expense or income) recognised in profit and loss and one component (remeasurements) of the change recognised in other comprehensive income.
- Under US GAAP, the change in the defined benefit plan net asset or liability is also recognised as a cost of the period with three components of the change (current service costs, interest expense on the beginning pension obligation, and expected return on plan assets) recognised in profit and loss and two components (past service costs and actuarial gains and losses) recognised in other comprehensive income.
- Solvency refers to a company's ability to meet its long-term debt obligations.

- In evaluating solvency, leverage ratios focus on the balance sheet and measure the amount of debt financing relative to equity financing.
- In evaluating solvency, coverage ratios focus on the income statement and cash flows and measure the ability of a company to cover its interest payments.

PROBLEMS

1. A company issues €1 million of bonds at face value. When the bonds are issued, the company will record a:
   A. cash inflow from investing activities.
   B. cash inflow from financing activities.
   C. cash inflow from operating activities.

2. At the time of issue of 4.50% coupon bonds, the effective interest rate was 5.00%. The bonds were *most likely* issued at:
   A. par.
   B. a discount.
   C. a premium.

3. Oil Exploration LLC paid $45,000 in printing, legal fees, commissions, and other costs associated with its recent bond issue. It is *most likely* to record these costs on its financial statements as:
   A. an asset under US GAAP and reduction of the carrying value of the debt under IFRS.
   B. a liability under US GAAP and reduction of the carrying value of the debt under IFRS.
   C. a cash outflow from investing activities under both US GAAP and IFRS.

4. On 1 January 2010, Elegant Fragrances Company issues £1,000,000 face value, five-year bonds with annual interest payments of £55,000 to be paid each 31 December. The market interest rate is 6.0 percent. Using the effective interest rate method of amortisation, Elegant Fragrances is *most likely* to record:
   A. an interest expense of £55,000 on its 2010 income statement.
   B. a liability of £982,674 on the 31 December 2010 balance sheet.
   C. a £58,736 cash outflow from operating activity on the 2010 statement of cash flows.

5. Consolidated Enterprises issues €10 million face value, five-year bonds with a coupon rate of 6.5 percent. At the time of issuance, the market interest rate is 6.0 percent. Using the effective interest rate method of amortisation, the carrying value after one year will be *closest* to:
   A. €10.17 million.
   B. €10.21 million.
   C. €10.28 million.

6. The management of Bank EZ repurchases its own bonds in the open market. They pay €6.5 million for bonds with a face value of €10.0 million and a carrying value of €9.8 million. The bank will *most likely* report:
   A. other comprehensive income of €3.3 million.
   B. other comprehensive income of €3.5 million.
   C. a gain of €3.3 million on the income statement.

7. Innovative Inventions, Inc. needs to raise €10 million. If the company chooses to issue zero-coupon bonds, its debt-to-equity ratio will *most likely*:
   A. rise as the maturity date approaches.
   B. decline as the maturity date approaches.
   C. remain constant throughout the life of the bond.

8. Fairmont Golf issued fixed rate debt when interest rates were 6 percent. Rates have since risen to 7 percent. Using only the carrying amount (based on historical cost) reported on the balance sheet to analyze the company's financial position would *most likely* cause an analyst to:
   A. overestimate Fairmont's economic liabilities.
   B. underestimate Fairmont's economic liabilities.
   C. underestimate Fairmont's interest coverage ratio.

9. Debt covenants are *least likely* to place restrictions on the issuer's ability to:
   A. pay dividends.
   B. issue additional debt.
   C. issue additional equity.

10. Compared to using a finance lease, a lessee that makes use of an operating lease will *most likely* report higher:
    A. debt.
    B. rent expense.
    C. cash flow from operating activity.

11. Which of the following is *most likely* a lessee's disclosure about operating leases?
    A. Lease liabilities.
    B. Future obligations by maturity.
    C. Net carrying amounts of leased assets.

12. For a lessor, the leased asset appears on the balance sheet and continues to be depreciated when the lease is classified as:
    A. a sales-type lease.
    B. an operating lease.
    C. a financing lease.

13. Under US GAAP, a lessor's reported revenues at lease inception will be *highest* if the lease is classified as:
    A. a sales-type lease.
    B. an operating lease.
    C. a direct financing lease.

14. A lessor will record interest income if a lease is classified as:
    A. a capital lease.
    B. an operating lease.
    C. either a capital or an operating lease.

15. Cavalier Copper Mines has $840 million in total liabilities and $520 million in shareholders' equity. It discloses operating lease commitments over the next five years with a present value of $100 million. If the lease commitments are treated as debt, the debt-to-total-capital ratio is *closest* to:
    A. 0.58.
    B. 0.62.
    C. 0.64.

16. Penben Corporation has a defined benefit pension plan. At 31 December, its pension obligation is €10 million and pension assets are €9 million. Under either IFRS or US GAAP, the reporting on the balance sheet would be *closest* to which of the following?

    A. €10 million is shown as a liability, and €9 million appears as an asset.

    B. €1 million is shown as a net pension obligation.

    C. Pension assets and obligations are not required to be shown on the balance sheet but only disclosed in footnotes.

CHAPTER 11

FINANCIAL
REPORTING QUALITY

LEARNING OUTCOMES

After completing this chapter, you will be able to do the following:

- distinguish between financial reporting quality and quality of reported results (including quality of earnings, cash flow, and balance sheet items);
- describe a spectrum for assessing financial reporting quality;
- distinguish between conservative and aggressive accounting;
- describe motivations that might cause management to issue financial reports that are not high quality;
- describe conditions that are conducive to issuing low-quality, or even fraudulent, financial reports;
- describe mechanisms that discipline financial reporting quality and the potential limitations of those mechanisms;
- describe presentation choices, including non-GAAP measures, that could be used to influence an analyst's opinion;
- describe accounting methods (choices and estimates) that could be used to manage earnings, cash flow, and balance sheet items;
- describe accounting warning signs and methods for detecting manipulation of information in financial reports.

SUMMARY OVERVIEW

- Financial reporting quality can be thought of as spanning a continuum from the highest (containing information that is relevant, correct, complete, and unbiased) to the lowest (containing information that is not just biased or incomplete but possibly pure fabrication).

- *Reporting quality*, the focus of this chapter, pertains to the information disclosed. High-quality reporting represents the economic reality of the company's activities during the reporting period and the company's financial condition at the end of the period.
- *Results quality* (commonly referred to as earnings quality) pertains to the earnings and cash generated by the company's actual economic activities and the resulting financial condition, relative to expectations of current and future financial performance.
- An aspect of financial reporting quality is the degree to which accounting choices are conservative or aggressive. "Aggressive" typically refers to choices that aim to enhance the company's reported performance and financial position by inflating the amount of revenues, earnings, and/or operating cash flow reported in the period; or by decreasing the amount of expenses reported in the period and/or the amount of debt reported on the balance sheet.
- Conservatism in financial reports can result from either (1) accounting standards that specifically require a conservative treatment of a transaction or an event or (2) judgments necessarily made by managers when applying accounting standards that result in more- or less-conservative results.
- An example of conservatism in the oil and gas industry is the revenue recognition accounting standard. This standard permits recognition of revenue only at time of shipment rather than closer to the time of actual value creation, which is the time of discovery.
- Managers may be motivated to issue less than high quality financial reports in order to mask poor performance, to boost the stock price, to increase personal compensation, and/or to avoid violation of debt covenants.
- Conditions that are conducive to the issuance of low-quality financial reports include cultural environment attributes that result in fewer or less transparent financial disclosures, book/ tax conformity that shifts emphasis toward legal compliance and away from fair presentation, and limited capital markets regulation.
- Mechanisms that discipline financial reporting quality include the free market and incentives for companies to minimize cost of capital, auditors, contract provisions specifically tailored to penalize misreporting, and enforcement by regulatory entities.
- Pro forma earnings (also commonly referred to as non-GAAP or non-IFRS earnings) adjust earnings as reported on the income statement. Pro forma earnings that exclude negative items are a hallmark of aggressive presentation choices.
- Companies are required to make additional disclosures when presenting any non-GAAP or non-IFRS metric.
- Managers' considerable flexibility in choosing their companies' accounting policies and in formulating estimates provides opportunities for aggressive accounting.
- Examples of accounting choices that affect earnings and balance sheets include inventory cost flow assumptions, estimates of uncollectible accounts receivable, estimated realizability of deferred tax assets, depreciation method, estimated salvage value of depreciable assets, and estimated useful life of depreciable assets.
- Cash from operations is a metric of interest to investors that can be enhanced by operating choices, such as stretching accounts payable, and potentially by classification choices.

PROBLEMS

1. The information provided by a low-quality financial report will *most likely*:
   A. decrease company value.
   B. indicate earnings are not sustainable.
   C. impede the assessment of earnings quality.

2. To properly assess a company's past performance, an analyst requires:
   A. high earnings quality.
   B. high financial reporting quality.
   C. both high earnings quality and high financial reporting quality.

3. Low quality earnings *most likely* reflect:
   A. low-quality financial reporting.
   B. company activities which are unsustainable.
   C. information that does not faithfully represent company activities.

4. Financial reports of the lowest level of quality reflect:
   A. fictitious events.
   B. biased accounting choices.
   C. accounting that is non-compliant with GAAP.

5. If a particular accounting choice is considered aggressive in nature, then the financial performance for the current period would *most likely*:
   A. be neutral.
   B. exhibit an upward bias.
   C. exhibit a downward bias.

6. Which of the following is *most likely* to reflect conservative accounting choices?
   A. Decreased reported earnings in later periods
   B. Increased reported earnings in the current period
   C. Increased debt reported on the balance sheet at the end of the current period

7. Which of the following statements *most likely* describes a situation that would motivate a manager to issue low-quality financial reports?
   A. The manager's compensation is tied to stock price performance.
   B. The manager has increased the market share of products significantly.
   C. The manager has brought the company's profitability to a level higher than competitors.

8. A company is experiencing a period of strong financial performance. In order to increase the likelihood of exceeding analysts' earnings forecasts in the next reporting period, the company would *most likely* undertake accounting choices that:
   A. inflate reported revenue in the current period.
   B. delay expense recognition in the current period.
   C. accelerate expense recognition in the current period.

9. Which of the following situations will *most likely* motivate managers to inflate earnings in the current period?
   A. Possibility of bond covenant violation
   B. Earnings in excess of analysts' forecasts
   C. Earnings that are greater than the previous year

10. Which of the following *best* describes an opportunity for management to issue low-quality financial reports?
    A. Ineffective board of directors
    B. Pressure to achieve some performance level
    C. Corporate concerns about financing in the future

11. An audit opinion of a company's financial reports is *most likely* intended to:
    A. detect fraud.
    B. reveal misstatements.
    C. assure that financial information is presented fairly.

12. If a company uses a non-GAAP financial measure in an SEC filing, then the company must:
    A. give more prominence to the non-GAAP measure if it is used in earnings releases.
    B. provide a reconciliation of the non-GAAP measure and equivalent GAAP measure.
    C. exclude charges requiring cash settlement from any non-GAAP liquidity measures.

13. A company wishing to increase earnings in the current period may choose to:
    A. decrease the useful life of depreciable assets.
    B. lower estimates of uncollectible accounts receivables.
    C. classify a purchase as an expense rather than a capital expenditure.

14. Bias in revenue recognition would *least likely* be suspected if:
    A. the firm engages in barter transactions.
    B. reported revenue is higher than the previous quarter.
    C. revenue is recognized before goods are shipped to customers.

15. Which of the following is an indication that a company may be recognizing revenue prematurely? Relative to its competitors, the company's:
    A. asset turnover is decreasing.
    B. receivables turnover is increasing.
    C. days sales outstanding is increasing.

16. Which of the following would *most likely* signal that a company may be using aggressive accrual accounting policies to shift current expenses to later periods? Over the last five-year period, the ratio of cash flow to net income has:
    A. increased each year.
    B. decreased each year.
    C. fluctuated from year to year.

CHAPTER 12

FINANCIAL STATEMENT ANALYSIS: APPLICATIONS

LEARNING OUTCOMES

After completing this chapter, you will be able to do the following:

- evaluate a company's past financial performance and explain how a company's strategy is reflected in past financial performance;
- forecast a company's future net income and cash flow;
- describe the role of financial statement analysis in assessing the credit quality of a potential debt investment;
- describe the use of financial statement analysis in screening for potential equity investments;
- explain appropriate analyst adjustments to a company's financial statements to facilitate comparison with another company.

SUMMARY OVERVIEW

- Evaluating a company's historical performance addresses not only what happened but also the causes behind the company's performance and how the performance reflects the company's strategy.
- The projection of a company's future net income and cash flow often begins with a top-down sales forecast in which the analyst forecasts industry sales and the company's market share. By projecting profit margins or expenses and the level of investment in working and fixed capital needed to support projected sales, the analyst can forecast net income and cash flow.

- Projections of future performance are needed for discounted cash flow valuation of equity and are often needed in credit analysis to assess a borrower's ability to repay interest and principal of a debt obligation.
- Credit analysis uses financial statement analysis to evaluate credit-relevant factors, including tolerance for leverage, operational stability, and margin stability.
- When ratios constructed from financial statement data and market data are used to screen for potential equity investments, fundamental decisions include which metrics to use as screens, how many metrics to include, what values of those metrics to use as cutoff points, and what weighting to give each metric.
- Analyst adjustments to a company's reported financial statements are sometimes necessary (e.g., when comparing companies that use different accounting methods or assumptions). Adjustments include those related to investments; inventory; property, plant, and equipment; goodwill; and off-balance-sheet financing.

PROBLEMS

1. Projecting profit margins into the future on the basis of past results would be *most* reliable when the company:
   A. is in the commodities business.
   B. operates in a single business segment.
   C. is a large, diversified company operating in mature industries.

2. Galambos Corporation had an average receivables collection period of 19 days in 2003. Galambos has stated that it wants to decrease its collection period in 2004 to match the industry average of 15 days. Credit sales in 2003 were $300 million, and analysts expect credit sales to increase to $400 million in 2004. To achieve the company's goal of decreasing the collection period, the change in the average accounts receivable balance from 2003 to 2004 that must occur is *closest* to:
   A. −$420,000.
   B. $420,000.
   C. $836,000.

3. Credit analysts are likely to consider which of the following in making a rating recommendation?
   A. Business risk but not financial risk
   B. Financial risk but not business risk
   C. Both business risk and financial risk

4. When screening for potential equity investments based on return on equity, to control risk, an analyst would be *most likely* to include a criterion that requires:
   A. positive net income.
   B. negative net income.
   C. negative shareholders' equity.

5. One concern when screening for stocks with low price-to-earnings ratios is that companies with low P/Es may be financially weak. What criterion might an analyst include to avoid inadvertently selecting weak companies?
   A. Net income less than zero

   B. Debt-to-total assets ratio below a certain cutoff point
   C. Current-year sales growth lower than prior-year sales growth

6. When a database eliminates companies that cease to exist because of a merger or bankruptcy, this can result in:
   A. look-ahead bias.
   B. back-testing bias.
   C. survivorship bias.

7. In a comprehensive financial analysis, financial statements should be:
   A. used as reported without adjustment.
   B. adjusted after completing ratio analysis.
   C. adjusted for differences in accounting standards, such as international financial reporting standards and US generally accepted accounting principles.

8. When comparing financial statements prepared under IFRS with those prepared under US GAAP, analysts may need to make adjustments related to:
   A. realized losses.
   B. unrealized gains and losses for trading securities.
   C. unrealized gains and losses for available-for-sale securities.

9. When comparing a US company that uses the last in, first out (LIFO) method of inventory with companies that prepare their financial statements under international financial reporting standards (IFRS), analysts should be aware that according to IFRS, the LIFO method of inventory:
   A. is never acceptable.
   B. is always acceptable.
   C. is acceptable when applied to finished goods inventory only.

10. An analyst is evaluating the balance sheet of a US company that uses last in, first out (LIFO) accounting for inventory. The analyst collects the following data:

	31 Dec 05	31 Dec 06
Inventory reported on balance sheet	$500,000	$600,000
LIFO reserve	$ 50,000	$70,000
Average tax rate	30%	30%

   After adjusting the amounts to convert to the first in, first out (FIFO) method, inventory at 31 December 2006 would be closest to:
   A. $600,000.
   B. $620,000.
   C. $670,000.

11. An analyst gathered the following data for a company ($ millions):

	31 Dec 2000	31 Dec 2001
Gross investment in fixed assets	$2.8	$2.8
Accumulated depreciation	$1.2	$1.6

The average age and average depreciable life of the company's fixed assets at the end of 2001 are *closest* to:

	Average Age	Average Depreciable Life
A.	1.75 years	7 years
B.	1.75 years	14 years
C.	4.00 years	7 years

12. To compute tangible book value, an analyst would
    A. add goodwill to stockholders' equity.
    B. add all intangible assets to stockholders' equity.
    C. subtract all intangible assets from stockholders' equity.

13. Which of the following is an off-balance-sheet financing technique? The use of
    A. capital leases.
    B. operating leases.
    C. the last in, first out inventory method.

14. To better evaluate the solvency of a company, an analyst would most likely add to total liabilities
    A. the present value of future capital lease payments.
    B. the total amount of future operating lease payments.
    C. the present value of future operating lease payments.

CHAPTER **13**

INCOME TAXES

LEARNING OUTCOMES

After completing this chapter, you will be able to do the following:

- describe the differences between accounting profit and taxable income, and define key terms, including deferred tax assets, deferred tax liabilities, valuation allowance, taxes payable, and income tax expense;
- explain how deferred tax liabilities and assets are created and the factors that determine how a company's deferred tax liabilities and assets should be treated for the purposes of financial analysis;
- calculate the tax base of a company's assets and liabilities;
- calculate income tax expense, income taxes payable, deferred tax assets, and deferred tax liabilities, and calculate and interpret the adjustment to the financial statements related to a change in the income tax rate;
- evaluate the impact of tax rate changes on a company's financial statements and ratios;
- distinguish between temporary and permanent differences in pre-tax accounting income and taxable income;
- describe the valuation allowance for deferred tax assets—when it is required and what impact it has on financial statements;
- compare a company's deferred tax items;
- analyze disclosures relating to deferred tax items and the effective tax rate reconciliation, and explain how information included in these disclosures affects a company's financial statements and financial ratios;
- identify the key provisions of and differences between income tax accounting under International Financial Reporting Standards (IFRS) and US generally accepted accounting principles (GAAP).

SUMMARY OVERVIEW

- Differences between the recognition of revenue and expenses for tax and accounting purposes may result in taxable income differing from accounting profit. The discrepancy is a result of different treatments of certain income and expenditure items.
- The tax base of an asset is the amount that will be deductible for tax purposes as an expense in the calculation of taxable income as the company expenses the tax basis of the asset. If the economic benefit will not be taxable, the tax base of the asset will be equal to the carrying amount of the asset.
- The tax base of a liability is the carrying amount of the liability less any amounts that will be deductible for tax purposes in the future. With respect to revenue received in advance, the tax base of such a liability is the carrying amount less any amount of the revenue that will not be taxable in the future.
- Temporary differences arise from recognition of differences in the tax base and carrying amount of assets and liabilities. The creation of a deferred tax asset or liability as a result of a temporary difference will only be allowed if the difference reverses itself at some future date and to the extent that it is expected that the balance sheet item will create future economic benefits for the company.
- Permanent differences result in a difference in tax and financial reporting of revenue (expenses) that will not be reversed at some future date. Because it will not be reversed at a future date, these differences do not constitute temporary differences and do not give rise to a deferred tax asset or liability.
- Current taxes payable or recoverable are based on the applicable tax rates on the balance sheet date of an entity; in contrast, deferred taxes should be measured at the tax rate that is expected to apply when the asset is realized or the liability settled.
- All unrecognized deferred tax assets and liabilities must be reassessed on the appropriate balance sheet date and measured against their probable future economic benefit.
- Deferred tax assets must be assessed for their prospective recoverability. If it is probable that they will not be recovered at all or partly, the carrying amount should be reduced. Under US GAAP, this is done through the use of a valuation allowance.

PROBLEMS

1. Using the straight-line method of depreciation for reporting purposes and accelerated depreciation for tax purposes would *most likely* result in a:
   A. valuation allowance.
   B. deferred tax asset.
   C. temporary difference.

2. In early 2009 Sanborn Company must pay the tax authority €37,000 on the income it earned in 2008. This amount was recorded on the company's 31 December 2008 financial statements as:
   A. taxes payable.
   B. income tax expense.
   C. a deferred tax liability.

3. Income tax expense reported on a company's income statement equals taxes payable, plus the net increase in:
   A. deferred tax assets and deferred tax liabilities.
   B. deferred tax assets, less the net increase in deferred tax liabilities.
   C. deferred tax liabilities, less the net increase in deferred tax assets.

4. Analysts should treat deferred tax liabilities that are expected to reverse as:
   A. equity.
   B. liabilities.
   C. neither liabilities nor equity.

5. Deferred tax liabilities should be treated as equity when:
   A. they are not expected to reverse.
   B. the timing of tax payments is uncertain.
   C. the amount of tax payments is uncertain.

6. When both the timing and amount of tax payments are uncertain, analysts should treat deferred tax liabilities as:
   A. equity.
   B. liabilities.
   C. neither liabilities nor equity.

7. When accounting standards require recognition of an expense that is not permitted under tax laws, the result is a:
   A. deferred tax liability.
   B. temporary difference.
   C. permanent difference.

8. When certain expenditures result in tax credits that directly reduce taxes, the company will *most likely* record:
   A. a deferred tax asset.
   B. a deferred tax liability.
   C. no deferred tax asset or liability.

9. When accounting standards require an asset to be expensed immediately but tax rules require the item to be capitalized and amortized, the company will *most likely* record:
   A. a deferred tax asset.
   B. a deferred tax liability.
   C. no deferred tax asset or liability.

10. A company incurs a capital expenditure that may be amortized over five years for accounting purposes, but over four years for tax purposes. The company will *most likely* record:
    A. a deferred tax asset.
    B. a deferred tax liability.
    C. no deferred tax asset or liability.

11. A company receives advance payments from customers that are immediately taxable but will not be recognized for accounting purposes until the company fulfills its obligation. The company will *most likely* record:
    A. a deferred tax asset.
    B. a deferred tax liability.
    C. no deferred tax asset or liability.

The following information relates to Questions 12–14

Note I
Income Taxes

The components of earnings before income taxes are as follows ($ thousands):

	2007	2006	2005
Earnings before income taxes:			
United States	$88,157	$75,658	$59,973
Foreign	116,704	113,509	94,760
Total	$204,861	$189,167	$154,733

The components of the provision for income taxes are as follows ($ thousands):

	2007	2006	2005
Income taxes			
Current:			
Federal	$30,632	$22,031	$18,959
Foreign	28,140	27,961	22,263
	$58,772	$49,992	$41,222
Deferred:			
Federal	($4,752)	$5,138	$2,336
Foreign	124	1,730	621
	(4,628)	6,868	2,957
Total	$54,144	$56,860	$44,179

12. In 2007, the company's US GAAP income statement recorded a provision for income taxes *closest* to:
    A. $30,632.
    B. $54,144.
    C. $58,772.

13. The company's effective tax rate was *highest* in:
    A. 2005.
    B. 2006.
    C. 2007.

14. Compared to the company's effective tax rate on US income, its effective tax rate on foreign income was:
    A. lower in each year presented.
    B. higher in each year presented.
    C. higher in some periods and lower in others.

15. Zimt AG presents its financial statements in accordance with US GAAP. In 2007, Zimt discloses a valuation allowance of $1,101 against total deferred tax assets of $19,201. In 2006, Zimt disclosed a valuation allowance of $1,325 against total deferred tax assets of $17,325. The change in the valuation allowance *most likely* indicates that Zimt's:
    A. deferred tax liabilities were reduced in 2007.
    B. expectations of future earning power has increased.
    C. expectations of future earning power has decreased.

16. Cinnamon, Inc. recorded a total deferred tax asset in 2007 of $12,301, offset by a $12,301 valuation allowance. Cinnamon *most likely*:
    A. fully utilized the deferred tax asset in 2007.
    B. has an equal amount of deferred tax assets and deferred tax liabilities.
    C. expects not to earn any taxable income before the deferred tax asset expires.

The following information relates to Questions 17–19

The tax effects of temporary differences that give rise to deferred tax assets and liabilities are as follows ($ thousands):

	2007	2006
Deferred tax assets:		
Accrued expenses	$8,613	$7,927
Tax credit and net operating loss carryforwards	2,288	2,554
LIFO and inventory reserves	5,286	4,327
Other	2,664	2,109
Deferred tax assets	18,851	16,917
Valuation allowance	(1,245)	(1,360)
Net deferred tax assets	$17,606	$15,557
Deferred tax liabilities:		
Depreciation and amortization	$(27,338)	$(29,313)
Compensation and retirement plans	(3,831)	(8,963)
Other	(1,470)	(764)
Deferred tax liabilities	(32,639)	(39,040)
Net deferred tax liability	$(15,033)	$(23,483)

17. A reduction in the statutory tax rate would *most likely* benefit the company's:
    A. income statement and balance sheet.
    B. income statement but not the balance sheet.
    C. balance sheet but not the income statement.

18. If the valuation allowance had been the same in 2007 as it was in 2006, the company would have reported $115 *higher*:
    A. net income.
    B. deferred tax assets.
    C. income tax expense.

19. Compared to the provision for income taxes in 2007, the company's cash tax payments were:
    A. lower.
    B. higher.
    C. the same.

The following information relates to Questions 20–22

A company's provision for income taxes resulted in effective tax rates attributable to loss from continuing operations before cumulative effect of change in accounting principles that varied from the statutory federal income tax rate of 34 percent, as summarized in the table below.

Year Ended 30 June	2007	2006	2005
Expected federal income tax expense (benefit) from continuing operations at 34 percent	($112,000)	$768,000	$685,000
Expenses not deductible for income tax purposes	357,000	32,000	51,000
State income taxes, net of federal benefit	132,000	22,000	100,000
Change in valuation allowance for deferred tax assets	(150,000)	(766,000)	(754,000)
Income tax expense	$227,000	$56,000	$82,000

20. In 2007, the company's net income (loss) was *closest* to:
    A. ($217,000).
    B. ($329,000).
    C. ($556,000).

21. The $357,000 adjustment in 2007 *most likely* resulted in:
    A. an increase in deferred tax assets.
    B. an increase in deferred tax liabilities.
    C. no change to deferred tax assets and liabilities.

22. Over the three years presented, changes in the valuation allowance for deferred tax assets were *most likely* indicative of:
    A. decreased prospect for future profitability.
    B. increased prospects for future profitability.
    C. assets being carried at a higher value than their tax base.

CHAPTER 14

EMPLOYEE COMPENSATION: POST-EMPLOYMENT AND SHARE-BASED

LEARNING OUTCOMES

After completing this chapter, you will be able to do the following:

- describe the types of post-employment benefit plans and implications for financial reports;
- explain and calculate measures of a defined benefit pension obligation (i.e., present value of the defined benefit obligation and projected benefit obligation) and net pension liability (or asset);
- describe the components of a company's defined benefit pension costs;
- explain and calculate the effect of a defined benefit plan's assumptions on the defined benefit obligation and periodic pension cost;
- explain and calculate how adjusting for items of pension and other post-employment benefits that are reported in the notes to the financial statements affects financial statements and ratios;
- interpret pension plan note disclosures including cash flow related information;
- explain issues associated with accounting for share-based compensation;
- explain how accounting for stock grants and stock options affects financial statements, and the importance of companies' assumptions in valuing these grants and options.

SUMMARY OVERVIEW

- Defined contribution pension plans specify (define) only the amount of contribution to the plan; the eventual amount of the pension benefit to the employee will depend on the value of an employee's plan assets at the time of retirement.

- Balance sheet reporting is less analytically relevant for defined contribution plans because companies make contributions to defined contribution plans as the expense arises and thus no liabilities accrue for that type of plan.
- Defined benefit pension plans specify (define) the amount of the pension benefit, often determined by a plan formula, under which the eventual amount of the benefit to the employee is a function of length of service and final salary.
- Defined benefit pension plan obligations are funded by the sponsoring company contributing assets to a pension trust, a separate legal entity. Differences exist in countries' regulatory requirements for companies to fund defined benefit pension plan obligations.
- Both IFRS and US GAAP require companies to report on their balance sheet a pension liability or asset equal to the projected benefit obligation minus the fair value of plan assets. The amount of a pension asset that can be reported is subject to a ceiling.
- Under IFRS, the components of periodic pension cost are recognised as follows: Service cost is recognised in P&L, net interest income/expense is recognised in P&L, and remeasurements are recognised in OCI and are not amortised to future P&L.
- Under US GAAP, the components of periodic pension cost recognised in P&L include current service costs, interest expense on the pension obligation, and expected returns on plan assets (which reduces the cost). Other components of periodic pension cost—including past service costs, actuarial gains and losses, and differences between expected and actual returns on plan assets—are recognised in OCI and amortised to future P&L.
- Estimates of the future obligation under defined benefit pension plans and other post-employment benefits are sensitive to numerous assumptions, including discount rates, assumed annual compensation increases, expected return on plan assets, and assumed health care cost inflation.
- Employee compensation packages are structured to fulfill varied objectives, including satisfying employees' needs for liquidity, retaining employees, and providing incentives to employees.
- Common components of employee compensation packages are salary, bonuses, and share-based compensation.
- Share-based compensation serves to align employees' interests with those of the shareholders. It includes stocks and stock options.
- Share-based compensation has the advantage of requiring no current-period cash outlays.
- Share-based compensation expense is reported at fair value under IFRS and US GAAP.
- The valuation technique, or option pricing model, that a company uses is an important choice in determining fair value and is disclosed.
- Key assumptions and input into option pricing models include such items as exercise price, stock price volatility, estimated life of each award, estimated number of options that will be forfeited, dividend yield, and the risk-free rate of interest. Certain assumptions are highly subjective, such as stock price volatility or the expected life of stock options, and can greatly change the estimated fair value and thus compensation expense.

PROBLEMS

Developed by Elaine Henry, CFA (Coral Gables, USA), and Elizabeth A. Gordon (Philadelphia, USA). Copyright © 2013 by CFA Institute.

The following information relates to Questions 1–7

Kensington plc, a hypothetical company based in the United Kingdom, offers its employees a defined benefit pension plan. Kensington complies with IFRS. The assumed discount rate that the company used in estimating the present value of its pension obligations was 5.48 percent. Information on Kensington's retirement plans is presented in Exhibit 1.

EXHIBIT 1   Kensington plc Defined Benefit Pension Plan

(in millions)	2010
Components of periodic benefit cost	
Service cost	£228
Net interest (income) expense	273
Remeasurements	−18
Periodic pension cost	£483
Change in benefit obligation	
Benefit obligations at beginning of year	£28,416
Service cost	228
Interest cost	1,557
Benefits paid	−1,322
Actuarial gain or loss	0
Benefit obligations at end of year	£28,879
Change in plan assets	
Fair value of plan assets at beginning of year	£23,432
Actual return on plan assets	1,302
Employer contributions	693
Benefits paid	−1,322
Fair value of plan assets at end of year	£24,105
Funded status at beginning of year	−£4,984
Funded status at end of year	−£4,774

1. At year-end 2010, £28,879 million represents:
   A. the funded status of the plan.
   B. the defined benefit obligation.
   C. the fair value of the plan's assets.

2. For the year 2010, the net interest expense of £273 represents the interest cost on the:
   A. ending benefit obligation.
   B. beginning benefit obligation.
   C. beginning net pension obligation.

3. For the year 2010, the remeasurement component of Kensington's periodic pension cost represents:
   A. the change in the net pension obligation.
   B. actuarial gains and losses on the pension obligation.
   C. actual return on plan assets minus the amount of return on plan assets included in the net interest expense.

4. Which of the following is *closest* to the actual rate of return on beginning plan assets and the rate of return on beginning plan assets that is included in the interest income/expense calculation?
   A. The actual rate of return was 5.56 percent, and the rate included in interest income/expense was 5.48 percent.
   B. The actual rate of return was 1.17 percent, and the rate included in interest income/expense was 5.48 percent.
   C. Both the actual rate of return and the rate included in interest income/expense were 5.48 percent.

5. Which component of Kensington's periodic pension cost would be shown in OCI rather than P&L?
   A. Service cost
   B. Net interest (income) expense
   C. Remeasurements

6. The relationship between the periodic pension cost and the plan's funded status is *best* expressed in which of the following?
   A. Periodic pension cost of –£483 = Ending funded status of –£4,774 – Employer contributions of £693 – Beginning funded status of –£4,984.
   B. Periodic pension cost of £1,322 = Benefits paid of £1,322.
   C. Periodic pension cost of £210 = Ending funded status of –£4,774 – Beginning funded status of –£4,984.

7. An adjustment to Kensington's statement of cash flows to reclassify the company's excess contribution for 2010 would *most likely* entail reclassifying £210 million (excluding income tax effects) as an outflow related to:
   A. investing activities rather than operating activities.
   B. financing activities rather than operating activities.
   C. operating activities rather than financing activities.

The following information relates to Questions 8–13

XYZ SA, a hypothetical company, offers its employees a defined benefit pension plan. Information on XYZ's retirement plans is presented in Exhibit 2. It also grants stock options to executives. Exhibit 3 contains information on the volatility assumptions used to value stock options.

EXHIBIT 2   XYZ SA Retirement Plan Information 2009

Employer contributions	1,000
Current service costs	200
Past service costs	120
Discount rate used to estimate plan liabilities	7.00%
Benefit obligation at beginning of year	42,000
Benefit obligation at end of year	41,720
Actuarial loss due to increase in plan obligation	460
Plan assets at beginning of year	39,000
Plan assets at end of year	38,700
Actual return on plan assets	2,700
Expected rate of return on plan assets	8.00%

EXHIBIT 3   XYZ SA Volatility Assumptions Used to Value Stock
Option Grants

Grant Year	Weighted Average Expected Volatility
2009 valuation assumptions	
2005–2009	21.50%
2008 valuation assumptions	
2004–2008	23.00%

8. The retirement benefits paid during the year were *closest* to:
   A. 280.
   B. 3,000.
   C. 4,000.

9. The total periodic pension cost is *closest* to:
   A. 320.
   B. 1,020.
   C. 1,320.

10. The amount of periodic pension cost that would be reported in P&L under IFRS is *closest* to:
    A. 20.
    B. 530.
    C. 1,020.

11. Assuming the company chooses not to immediately recognise the actuarial loss and assuming there is no amortisation of past service costs or actuarial gains and losses, the amount of periodic pension cost that would be reported in P&L under US GAAP is *closest* to:
    A. 20.
    B. 59.
    C. 530.

12. Under IFRS, the amount of periodic pension cost that would be reported in OCI is *closest*
    to:
    A. 20.
    B. 490.
    C. 1,020.

13. Compared to 2009 net income as reported, if XYZ had used the same expected volatil-
    ity assumption for its 2009 option grants that it had used in 2008, its 2009 net income
    would have been:
    A. lower.
    B. higher.
    C. the same.

The following information relates to Questions 14–19

Stereo Warehouse is a US retailer that offers employees a defined benefit pension plan and
stock options as part of its compensation package. Stereo Warehouse prepares its financial
statements in accordance with US GAAP.

Peter Friedland, CFA, is an equity analyst concerned with earnings quality. He is particularly interested in whether the discretionary assumptions the company is making regarding
compensation plans are contributing to the recent earnings growth at Stereo Warehouse. He
gathers information from the company's regulatory filings regarding the pension plan assumptions in Exhibit 4 and the assumptions related to option valuation in Exhibit 5.

EXHIBIT 4   Assumptions Used for Stereo Warehouse Defined Benefit Plan

	2009	2008	2007
Expected long-term rate of return on plan assets	6.06%	6.14%	6.79%
Discount rate	4.85	4.94	5.38
Estimated future salary increases	4.00	4.44	4.25
Inflation	3.00	2.72	2.45

EXHIBIT 5   Option Valuation Assumptions

	2009	**2008**	**2007**
Risk-free rate	4.6%	3.8%	2.4%
Expected life	5.0 yrs	4.5 yrs	5.0 yrs
Dividend yield	1.0%	0.0%	0.0%
Expected volatility	29%	31%	35%

14. Compared to the 2009 reported financial statements, if Stereo Warehouse had used the
    same expected long-term rate of return on plan assets assumption in 2009 as it used in
    2007, its year-end 2009 pension obligation would *most likely* have been:
    A. lower.
    B. higher.
    C. the same.

15. Compared to the reported 2009 financial statements, if Stereo Warehouse had used the same discount rate as it used in 2007, it would have *most likely* reported lower:
    A. net income.
    B. total liabilities.
    C. cash flow from operating activities.

16. Compared to the assumptions Stereo Warehouse used to compute its periodic pension cost in 2008, earnings in 2009 were *most favorably* affected by the change in the:
    A. discount rate.
    B. estimated future salary increases.
    C. expected long-term rate of return on plan assets.

17. Compared to the pension assumptions Stereo Warehouse used in 2008, which of the following pairs of assumptions used in 2009 is *most likely* internally inconsistent?
    A. Estimated future salary increases, inflation
    B. Discount rate, estimated future salary increases
    C. Expected long-term rate of return on plan assets, discount rate

18. Compared to the reported 2009 financial statements, if Stereo Warehouse had used the 2007 expected volatility assumption to value its employee stock options, it would have *most likely* reported higher:
    A. net income.
    B. compensation expense.
    C. deferred compensation liability.

19. Compared to the assumptions Stereo Warehouse used to value stock options in 2008, earnings in 2009 were most favorably affected by the change in the:
    A. expected life.
    B. risk-free rate.
    C. dividend yield.

CHAPTER 15

INTERCORPORATE INVESTMENTS

LEARNING OUTCOMES

After completing this chapter, you will be able to do the following:

- describe the classification, measurement, and disclosure under International Financial Reporting Standards (IFRS) for 1) investments in financial assets, 2) investments in associates, 3) joint ventures, 4) business combinations, and 5) special purpose and variable interest entities;
- distinguish between IFRS and US GAAP in the classification, measurement, and disclosure of investments in financial assets, investments in associates, joint ventures, business combinations, and special purpose and variable interest entities;
- analyze how different methods used to account for intercorporate investments affect financial statements and ratios.

SUMMARY OVERVIEW

- Investments in financial assets are those in which the investor has no significant influence. They can be measured and reported as
  - Fair value through profit or loss.
  - Fair value through other comprehensive income.
  - Amortized cost.
  IFRS and US GAAP treat investments in financial assets in a similar manner.
- Investments in associates and joint ventures are those in which the investor has significant influence, but not control, over the investee's business activities. Because the investor can exert significant influence over financial and operating policy decisions, IFRS and US GAAP require the equity method of accounting because it provides a more objective basis for reporting investment income.

- The equity method requires the investor to recognize income as earned rather than when dividends are received.
- The equity investment is carried at cost, plus its share of post-acquisition income (after adjustments) less dividends received.
- The equity investment is reported as a single line item on the balance sheet and on the income statement.
- Current IFRS and US GAAP accounting standards require the use of the acquisition method to account for business combinations. Fair value of the consideration given is the appropriate measurement for identifiable assets and liabilities acquired in the business combination.
- Goodwill is the difference between the acquisition value and the fair value of the target's identifiable net tangible and intangible assets. Because it is considered to have an indefinite life, it is not amortized. Instead, it is evaluated at least annually for impairment. Impairment losses are reported on the income statement. IFRS uses a one-step approach to determine and measure the impairment loss, whereas US GAAP uses a two-step approach.
- If the acquiring company acquires less than 100%, non-controlling (minority) shareholders' interests are reported on the consolidated financial statements. IFRS allows the non-controlling interest to be measured at either its fair value (full goodwill) or at the non-controlling interest's proportionate share of the acquiree's identifiable net assets (partial goodwill). US GAAP requires the non-controlling interest to be measured at fair value (full goodwill).
- Consolidated financial statements are prepared in each reporting period.
- Special purpose (SPEs) and variable interest entities (VIEs) are required to be consolidated by the entity which is expected to absorb the majority of the expected losses or receive the majority of expected residual benefits.

PROBLEMS

The following information relates to Questions 1–6

Cinnamon, Inc. is a diversified manufacturing company headquartered in the United Kingdom. It complies with IFRS. In 2009, Cinnamon held a 19 percent passive equity ownership interest in Cambridge Processing that was classified as available-for-sale. During the year, the value of this investment rose by £2 million. In December 2009, Cinnamon announced that it would be increasing its ownership interest to 50 percent effective 1 January 2010 through a cash purchase. Cinnamon and Cambridge have no intercompany transactions.

Peter Lubbock, an analyst following both Cinnamon and Cambridge, is curious how the increased stake will affect Cinnamon's consolidated financial statements. He asks Cinnamon's CFO how the company will account for the investment, and is told that the decision has not yet been made. Lubbock decides to use his existing forecasts for both companies' financial statements to compare the outcomes of alternative accounting treatments.

Lubbock assembles abbreviated financial statement data for Cinnamon (Exhibit 1) and Cambridge (Exhibit 2) for this purpose.

EXHIBIT 1   Selected Financial Statement Information for
Cinnamon, Inc. (£ Millions)

Year ending 31 December	2009	2010*
Revenue	1,400	1,575
Operating income	126	142
Net income	62	69
31 December	**2009**	**2010***
Total assets	1,170	1,317
Shareholders' equity	616	685

*Estimates made prior to announcement of increased stake in Cambridge.

EXHIBIT 2   Selected Financial Statement Information for
Cambridge Processing (£ Millions)

Year ending 31 December	2009	2010*
Revenue	1,000	1,100
Operating income	80	88
Net income	40	44
Dividends paid	20	22
31 December	**2009**	**2010***
Total assets	800	836
Shareholders' equity	440	462

*Estimates made prior to announcement of increased stake by Cinnamon.

1. In 2009, Cinnamon's earnings before taxes includes a contribution (in £ millions) from its investment in Cambridge Processing that is *closest* to:
   A. £3.8.
   B. £5.8.
   C. £7.6.

2. In 2010, if Cinnamon is deemed to have control over Cambridge, it will *most likely* account for its investment in Cambridge using:
   A. the equity method.
   B. the acquisition method.
   C. proportionate consolidation.

3. At 31 December 2010, Cinnamon's shareholders' equity on its balance sheet would *most likely* be:
   A. highest if Cinnamon is deemed to have control of Cambridge.
   B. independent of the accounting method used for the investment in Cambridge.
   C. highest if Cinnamon is deemed to have significant influence over Cambridge.

4. In 2010, Cinnamon's net profit margin would be *highest* if:
   A. it is deemed to have control of Cambridge.
   B. it had not increased its stake in Cambridge.
   C. it is deemed to have significant influence over Cambridge.

5. At 31 December 2010, assuming control and recognition of goodwill, Cinnamon's reported debt to equity ratio will *most likely* be highest if it accounts for its investment in Cambridge using the:
   A. equity method.
   B. full goodwill method.
   C. partial goodwill method.

6. Compared to Cinnamon's operating margin in 2009, if it is deemed to have control of Cambridge, its operating margin in 2010 will *most likely* be:
   A. lower.
   B. higher.
   C. the same.

The following information relates to Questions 7–12

Zimt, AG is a consumer products manufacturer headquartered in Austria. It complies with IFRS. In 2009, Zimt held a 10 percent passive stake in Oxbow Limited that was classified as held for trading securities. During the year, the value of this stake declined by €3 million. In December 2009, Zimt announced that it would be increasing its ownership to 50 percent effective 1 January 2010.

Franz Gelblum, an analyst following both Zimt and Oxbow, is curious how the increased stake will affect Zimt's consolidated financial statements. Because Gelblum is uncertain how the company will account for the increased stake, he uses his existing forecasts for both companies' financial statements to compare various alternative outcomes.

Gelblum gathers abbreviated financial statement data for Zimt (Exhibit 1) and Oxbow (Exhibit 2) for this purpose.

EXHIBIT 1   Selected Financial Statement Estimates for Zimt AG (€ Millions)

Year ending 31 December	2009	2010*
Revenue	1,500	1,700
Operating income	135	153
Net income	66	75
31 December	2009	2010*
Total assets	1,254	1,421
Shareholders' equity	660	735

*Estimates made prior to announcement of increased stake in Oxbow.

EXHIBIT 2   Selected Financial Statement Estimates for Oxbow Limited (€ Millions)

Year ending 31 December	2009	2010*
Revenue	1,200	1,350
Operating income	120	135
Net income	60	68
Dividends paid	20	22
31 December	2009	2010*
Total assets	1,200	1,283
Shareholders' equity	660	706

*Estimates made prior to announcement of increased stake by Zimt.

7. In 2009, Zimt's earnings before taxes includes a contribution (in € millions) from its investment in Oxbow Limited *closest* to:
   A. (€0.6) million.
   B. (€1.0) million.
   C. €2.0 million.

8. At 31 December 2010, Zimt's total assets balance would *most likely* be:
   A. highest if Zimt is deemed to have control of Oxbow.
   B. highest if Zimt is deemed to have significant influence over Oxbow.
   C. unaffected by the accounting method used for the investment in Oxbow.

9. Based on Gelblum's estimates, if Zimt is deemed to have significant influence over Oxbow, its 2010 net income (in € millions) would be *closest* to:
   A. €75.
   B. €109.
   C. €143.

10. Based on Gelblum's estimates, if Zimt is deemed to have joint control of Oxbow, and Zimt uses the proportionate consolidation method, its 31 December 2010 total liabilities (in € millions) will *most likely* be *closest* to:
    A. €686.
    B. €975.
    C. €1,263.

11. Based on Gelblum's estimates, if Zimt is deemed to have control over Oxbow, its 2010 consolidated sales (in € millions) will be *closest* to:
    A. €1,700.
    B. €2,375.
    C. €3,050.

12. Based on Gelblum's estimates, Zimt's net income in 2010 will *most likely* be:
    A. highest if Zimt is deemed to have control of Oxbow.
    B. highest if Zimt is deemed to have significant influence over Oxbow.
    C. independent of the accounting method used for the investment in Oxbow.

The following information relates to Questions 13–18

Burton Howard, CFA, is an equity analyst with Maplewood Securities. Howard is preparing a research report on Confabulated Materials, SA, a publicly traded company based in France that complies with IFRS. As part of his analysis, Howard has assembled data gathered from the financial statement footnotes of Confabulated's 2009 Annual Report and from discussions with company management. Howard is concerned about the effect of this information on Confabulated's future earnings.

Information about Confabulated's investment portfolio for the years ended 31 December 2008 and 2009 is presented in Exhibit 1. As part of his research, Howard is considering the possible effect on reported income of Confabulated's accounting classification for fixed income investments.

EXHIBIT 1 Confabulated's Investment Portfolio (€ Thousands)

Characteristic	Bugle AG	Cathay Corp	Dumas SA
Classification	Available-for-sale	Held-to-maturity	Held-to-maturity
Cost*	€25,000	€40,000	€50,000
Market value, 31 December 2008	29,000	38,000	54,000
Market value, 31 December 2009	28,000	37,000	55,000

*All securities were acquired at par value.

In addition, Confabulated's annual report discusses a transaction under which receivables were securitized through a special purpose entity (SPE) for Confabulated's benefit.

13. The balance sheet carrying value of Confabulated's investment portfolio (in € thousands) at 31 December 2009 is *closest* to:
    A. 112,000.
    B. 115,000.
    C. 118,000.

14. The balance sheet carrying value of Confabulated's investment portfolio at 31 December 2009 would have been higher if which of the securities had been reclassified as a held for trading security?
    A. Bugle.
    B. Cathay.
    C. Dumas.

15. Compared to Confabulated's reported interest income in 2009, if Dumas had been classified as available-for-sale, the interest income would have been:
    A. lower.
    B. the same.
    C. higher.

16. Compared to Confabulated's reported earnings before taxes in 2009, if Bugle had been classified as a held for trading security, the earnings before taxes (in € thousands) would have been:
    A. the same.
    B. €1,000 lower.
    C. €3,000 higher.

17. Confabulated's reported interest income would be lower if the cost was the same but the par value (in € thousands) of:
    A. Bugle was €28,000.
    B. Cathay was €37,000.
    C. Dumas was €55,000.

18. Confabulated's special purpose entity is *most likely* to be:
    A. held off-balance sheet.
    B. consolidated on Confabulated's financial statements.
    C. consolidated on Confabulated's financial statements only if it is a "qualifying SPE."

The following information relates to Questions 19–24

BetterCare Hospitals, Inc. operates a chain of hospitals throughout the United States. The company has been expanding by acquiring local hospitals. Its largest acquisition, that of State-wide Medical, was made in 2001 under the pooling of interests method. BetterCare complies with US GAAP.

BetterCare is currently forming a 50/50 joint venture with Supreme Healthcare under which the companies will share control of several hospitals. BetterCare plans to use the equity method to account for the joint venture. Supreme Healthcare complies with IFRS and will use the proportionate consolidation method to account for the joint venture.

Erik Ohalin is an equity analyst who covers both companies. He has estimated the joint venture's financial information for 2010 in order to prepare his estimates of each company's earnings and financial performance. This information is presented in Exhibit 1.

EXHIBIT 1   Selected Financial Statement Forecasts for Joint Venture ($ Millions)

Year ending 31 December	2010
Revenue	1,430
Operating income	128
Net income	62
31 December	2010
Total assets	1,500
Shareholders' equity	740

Supreme Healthcare recently announced it had formed a special purpose entity through which it plans to sell up to $100 million of its accounts receivable. Supreme Healthcare has no voting interest in the SPE, but it is expected to absorb any losses that it may incur. Ohalin wants to estimate the impact this will have on Supreme Healthcare's consolidated financial statements.

19. Compared to accounting principles currently in use, the pooling method BetterCare used for its Statewide Medical acquisition has *most likely* caused its reported:
    A. revenue to be higher.
    B. total equity to be lower.
    C. total assets to be higher.

20. Based on Ohalin's estimates, the amount of joint venture revenue (in $ millions) included on BetterCare's consolidated 2010 financial statements should be *closest* to:
    A. $0.
    B. $715.
    C. $1,430.

21. Based on Ohalin's estimates, the amount of joint venture net income included on the consolidated financial statements of each venturer will *most likely* be:
    A. higher for BetterCare.
    B. higher for Supreme Healthcare.
    C. the same for both BetterCare and Supreme Healthcare.

22. Based on Ohalin's estimates, the amount of the joint venture's 31 December 2010 total assets (in $ millions) that will be included on Supreme Healthcare's consolidated financial statements will be *closest* to:
    A. $0.
    B. $750.
    C. $1,500.

23. Based on Ohalin's estimates, the amount of joint venture shareholders' equity at 31 December 2010 included on the consolidated financial statements of each venturer will *most likely* be:
    A. higher for BetterCare.
    B. higher for Supreme Healthcare.
    C. the same for both BetterCare and Supreme Healthcare.

24. If Supreme Healthcare sells its receivables to the SPE, its consolidated financial results will *most likely* show:
    A. a higher revenue for 2010.
    B. the same cash balance at 31 December 2010.
    C. the same accounts receivable balance at 31 December 2010.

The following information relates to Questions 25–30

Percy Byron, CFA, is an equity analyst with a UK-based investment firm. One firm Byron follows is NinMount PLC, a UK-based company. On 31 December 2008, NinMount paid £320 million to purchase a 50 percent stake in Boswell Company. The excess of the purchase price over the fair value of Boswell's net assets was attributable to previously unrecorded licenses. These licenses were estimated to have an economic life of six years. The fair value of Boswell's assets and liabilities other than licenses was equal to their recorded book values. NinMount and Boswell both use the pound sterling as their reporting currency and prepare their financial statements in accordance with IFRS.

Byron is concerned whether the investment should affect his "buy" rating on NinMount common stock. He knows NinMount could choose one of several accounting methods to report the results of its investment, but NinMount has not announced which method it will use. Byron forecasts that both companies' 2009 financial results (excluding any merger accounting adjustments) will be identical to those of 2008.

NinMount's and Boswell's condensed income statements for the year ended 31 December 2008, and condensed balance sheets at 31 December 2008, are presented in Exhibits 1 and 2, respectively.

EXHIBIT 1   NinMount PLC and Boswell Company Income Statements for the Year Ended
31 December 2008 (£ millions)

	NinMount	Boswell
Net sales	950	510
Cost of goods sold	(495)	(305)
Selling expenses	(50)	(15)
Administrative expenses	(136)	(49)
Depreciation & amortization expense	(102)	(92)
Interest expense	(42)	(32)
Income before taxes	125	17
Income tax expense	(50)	(7)
Net income	75	10

EXHIBIT 2   NinMount PLC and Boswell Company Balance Sheets at 31 December 2008 (£ millions)

	NinMount	Boswell
Cash	50	20
Receivables—net	70	45
Inventory	130	75
Total current assets	250	140
Property, plant, & equipment—net	1,570	930
Investment in Boswell	320	—
Total assets	2,140	1,070
Current liabilities	110	90
Long-term debt	600	400
Total liabilities	710	490
Common stock	850	535
Retained earnings	580	45
Total equity	1,430	580
Total liabilities and equity	2,140	1,070

Note: Balance sheets reflect the purchase price paid by NinMount, but do not yet consider the impact of the accounting method choice.

25. NinMount's current ratio on 31 December 2008 *most likely* will be highest if the results of the acquisition are reported using:
    A. the equity method.
    B. consolidation with full goodwill.
    C. consolidation with partial goodwill.

26. NinMount's long-term debt to equity ratio on 31 December 2008 *most likely* will be lowest if the results of the acquisition are reported using:
    A. the equity method.
    B. consolidation with full goodwill.
    C. consolidation with partial goodwill.

27. Based on Byron's forecast, if NinMount deems it has acquired control of Boswell, NinMount's consolidated 2009 depreciation and amortization expense (in £ millions) will be *closest* to:
    A. 102.
    B. 148.
    C. 204.

28. Based on Byron's forecast, NinMount's net profit margin for 2009 *most likely* will be highest if the results of the acquisition are reported using:
    A. the equity method.
    B. consolidation with full goodwill.
    C. consolidation with partial goodwill.

29. Based on Byron's forecast, NinMount's 2009 return on beginning equity *most likely* will be the same under:
    A. either of the consolidations, but different under the equity method.
    B. the equity method, consolidation with full goodwill, and consolidation with partial goodwill.
    C. none of the equity method, consolidation with full goodwill, or consolidation with partial goodwill.

30. Based on Byron's forecast, NinMount's 2009 total asset turnover ratio on beginning assets under the equity method is *most likely*:
    A. lower than if the results are reported using consolidation.
    B. the same as if the results are reported using consolidation.
    C. higher than if the results are reported using consolidation.

CHAPTER 16

MULTINATIONAL OPERATIONS

LEARNING OUTCOMES

After completing this chapter, you will be able to do the following:

- distinguish among presentation (reporting) currency, functional currency, and local currency;
- describe foreign currency transaction exposure, including accounting for and disclosures about foreign currency transaction gains and losses;
- analyze how changes in exchange rates affect the translated sales of the subsidiary and parent company;
- compare the current rate method and the temporal method, evaluate how each affects the parent company's balance sheet and income statement, and determine which method is appropriate in various scenarios;
- calculate the translation effects and evaluate the translation of a subsidiary's balance sheet and income statement into the parent company's presentation currency;
- analyze how the current rate method and the temporal method affect financial statements and ratios;
- analyze how alternative translation methods for subsidiaries operating in hyperinflationary economies affect financial statements and ratios;
- describe how multinational operations affect a company's effective tax rate;
- explain how changes in the components of sales affect earnings sustainability;
- analyze how currency fluctuations potentially affect financial results, given a company's countries of operation.

SUMMARY OVERVIEW

- The local currency is the national currency of the country where an entity is located. The functional currency is the currency of the primary economic environment in which an entity operates. Normally, the local currency is an entity's functional currency. For accounting purposes, any currency other than an entity's functional currency is a foreign currency for that entity. The currency in which financial statement amounts are presented is known as the presentation currency. In most cases, the presentation currency will be the same as the local currency.

- When an export sale (import purchase) on an account is denominated in a foreign currency, the sales revenue (inventory) and foreign currency account receivable (account payable) are translated into the seller's (buyer's) functional currency using the exchange rate on the transaction date. Any change in the functional currency value of the foreign currency account receivable (account payable) that occurs between the transaction date and the settlement date is recognized as a foreign currency transaction gain or loss in net income.

- If a balance sheet date falls between the transaction date and the settlement date, the foreign currency account receivable (account payable) is translated at the exchange rate at the balance sheet date. The change in the functional currency value of the foreign currency account receivable (account payable) is recognized as a foreign currency transaction gain or loss in income. Analysts should understand that these gains and losses are unrealized at the time they are recognized and might or might not be realized when the transactions are settled.

- A foreign currency transaction gain arises when an entity has a foreign currency receivable and the foreign currency strengthens or it has a foreign currency payable and the foreign currency weakens. A foreign currency transaction loss arises when an entity has a foreign currency receivable and the foreign currency weakens or it has a foreign currency payable and the foreign currency strengthens.

- Companies must disclose the net foreign currency gain or loss included in income. They may choose to report foreign currency transaction gains and losses as a component of operating income or as a component of non-operating income. If two companies choose to report foreign currency transaction gains and losses differently, operating profit and operating profit margin might not be directly comparable between the two companies.

- To prepare consolidated financial statements, foreign currency financial statements of foreign operations must be translated into the parent company's presentation currency. The major conceptual issues related to this translation process are, What is the appropriate exchange rate for translating each financial statement item, and how should the resulting translation adjustment be reflected in the consolidated financial statements? Two different translation methods are used worldwide.

- Under the current rate method, assets and liabilities are translated at the current exchange rate, equity items are translated at historical exchange rates, and revenues and expenses are translated at the exchange rate that existed when the underlying transaction occurred. For practical reasons, an average exchange rate is often used to translate income items.

- Under the temporal method, monetary assets (and non-monetary assets measured at current value) and monetary liabilities (and non-monetary liabilities measured at current value) are translated at the current exchange rate. Non-monetary assets and liabilities not measured at current value and equity items are translated at historical exchange rates.

Revenues and expenses, other than those expenses related to non-monetary assets, are translated at the exchange rate that existed when the underlying transaction occurred. Expenses related to non-monetary assets are translated at the exchange rates used for the related assets.

- Under both IFRS and US GAAP, the functional currency of a foreign operation determines the method to be used in translating its foreign currency financial statements into the parent's presentation currency and whether the resulting translation adjustment is recognized in income or as a separate component of equity.

- The foreign currency financial statements of a foreign operation that has a foreign currency as its functional currency are translated using the current rate method, and the translation adjustment is accumulated as a separate component of equity. The cumulative translation adjustment related to a specific foreign entity is transferred to net income when that entity is sold or otherwise disposed of. The balance sheet risk exposure associated with the current rate method is equal to the foreign subsidiary's net asset position.

- The foreign currency financial statements of a foreign operation that has the parent's presentation currency as its functional currency are translated using the temporal method, and the translation adjustment is included as a gain or loss in income. US GAAP refer to this process as remeasurement. The balance sheet exposure associated with the temporal method is equal to the foreign subsidiary's net monetary asset/liability position (adjusted for non-monetary items measured at current value).

- IFRS and US GAAP differ with respect to the translation of foreign currency financial statements of foreign operations located in a highly inflationary country. Under IFRS, the foreign currency statements are first restated for local inflation and then translated using the current exchange rate. Under US GAAP, the foreign currency financial statements are translated using the temporal method, with no restatement for inflation.

- Applying different translation methods for a given foreign operation can result in very different amounts reported in the parent's consolidated financial statements.

- Companies must disclose the total amount of translation gain or loss reported in income and the amount of translation adjustment included in a separate component of stockholders' equity. Companies are not required to separately disclose the component of translation gain or loss arising from foreign currency transactions and the component arising from application of the temporal method.

- Disclosures related to translation adjustments reported in equity can be used to include these as gains and losses in determining an adjusted amount of income following a clean-surplus approach to income measurement.

- Foreign currency translation rules are well established in both IFRS and US GAAP. Fortunately, except for the treatment of foreign operations located in highly inflationary countries, the two sets of standards have no major differences in this area. The ability to understand the impact of foreign currency translation on the financial results of a company using IFRS should apply equally well in the analysis of financial statements prepared in accordance with US GAAP.

- An analyst can obtain information about the tax impact of multinational operations from companies' disclosure on effective tax rates.

- For a multinational company, sales growth is driven not only by changes in volume and price but also by changes in the exchange rates between the reporting currency and the currency in which sales are made. Arguably, growth in sales that comes from changes in volume or price is more sustainable than growth in sales that comes from changes in exchange rates.

PROBLEMS

Practice Problems and Solutions: *International Financial Statement Analysis*, by Thomas R. Robinson, CFA, Jan Hendrik van Greuning, CFA, Elaine Henry, CFA, and Michael A. Broihahn, CFA. Copyright © 2013 by CFA Institute.

The following information relates to Questions 1–6

Pedro Ruiz is an analyst for a credit rating agency. One of the companies he follows, Eurexim SA, is based in France and complies with International Financial Reporting Standards (IFRS). Ruiz has learned that Eurexim used EUR220 million of its own cash and borrowed an equal amount to open a subsidiary in Ukraine. The funds were converted into hryvnia (UAH) on 31 December 20X1 at an exchange rate of EUR1.00 = UAH6.70 and used to purchase UAH1,500 million in fixed assets and UAH300 of inventories.

Ruiz is concerned about the effect that the subsidiary's results might have on Eurexim's consolidated financial statements. He calls Eurexim's Chief Financial Officer, but learns little. Eurexim is not willing to share sales forecasts and has not even made a determination as to the subsidiary's functional currency.

Absent more useful information, Ruiz decides to explore various scenarios to determine the potential impact on Eurexim's consolidated financial statements. Ukraine is not currently in a hyperinflationary environment, but Ruiz is concerned that this situation could change. Ruiz also believes the euro will appreciate against the hryvnia for the foreseeable future.

1. If Ukraine's economy becomes highly inflationary, Eurexim will *most likely* translate inventory by:
   A. restating for inflation and using the temporal method.
   B. restating for inflation and using the current exchange rate.
   C. using the temporal method with no restatement for inflation.

2. Given Ruiz's belief about the direction of exchange rates, Eurexim's gross profit margin would be *highest* if it accounts for the Ukraine subsidiary's inventory using:
   A. FIFO and the temporal method.
   B. FIFO and the current rate method.
   C. weighted-average cost and the temporal method.

3. If the euro is chosen as the Ukraine subsidiary's functional currency, Eurexim will translate its fixed assets using the:
   A. average rate for the reporting period.
   B. rate in effect when the assets were purchased.
   C. rate in effect at the end of the reporting period.

4. If the euro is chosen as the Ukraine subsidiary's functional currency, Eurexim will translate its accounts receivable using the:
   A. rate in effect at the transaction date.
   B. average rate for the reporting period.
   C. rate in effect at the end of the reporting period.

5. If the hryvnia is chosen as the Ukraine subsidiary's functional currency, Eurexim will translate its inventory using the:
   A. average rate for the reporting period.
   B. rate in effect at the end of the reporting period.
   C. rate in effect at the time the inventory was purchased.

6. Based on the information available and Ruiz's expectations regarding exchange rates, if the hryvnia is chosen as the Ukraine subsidiary's functional currency, Eurexim will *most likely* report:
   A. an addition to the cumulative translation adjustment.
   B. a translation gain or loss as a component of net income.
   C. a subtraction from the cumulative translation adjustment.

The following information relates to Questions 7–12

Consolidated Motors is a US-based corporation that sells mechanical engines and components used by electric utilities. Its Canadian subsidiary, Consol-Can, operates solely in Canada. It was created on 31 December 20X1, and Consolidated Motors determined at that time that it should use the US dollar as its functional currency.

Chief Financial Officer Monica Templeton was asked to explain to the board of directors how exchange rates affect the financial statements of both Consol-Can and the consolidated financial statements of Consolidated Motors. For the presentation, Templeton collects Consol-Can's balance sheets for the years ended 20X1 and 20X2 (Exhibit 1), as well as relevant exchange rate information (Exhibit 2).

EXHIBIT 1   Consol-Can Condensed Balance Sheet for Fiscal Years Ending 31 December (C$ millions)

Account	20X2	20X1
Cash	135	167
Accounts receivable	98	—
Inventory	77	30
Fixed assets	100	100
Accumulated depreciation	(10)	—
Total assets	400	297
Accounts payable	77	22
Long-term debt	175	175
Common stock	100	100
Retained earnings	48	—
Total liabilities and shareholders' equity	400	297

EXHIBIT 2   Exchange Rate Information

	US$/C$
Rate on 31 December 20X1	0.86
Average rate in 20X2	0.92
Weighted-average rate for inventory purchases	0.92
Rate on 31 December 20X2	0.95

Templeton explains that Consol-Can uses the FIFO inventory accounting method and that purchases of C$300 million and the sell-through of that inventory occurred evenly throughout 20X2. Her presentation includes reporting the translated amounts in US dollars for each item, as well as associated translation-related gains and losses. The board responds with several questions.

• Would there be a reason to change the functional currency to the Canadian dollar?
• Would there be any translation effects for Consolidated Motors if the functional currency for Consol-Can were changed to the Canadian dollar?
• Would a change in the functional currency have any impact on financial statement ratios for the parent company?
• What would be the balance sheet exposure to translation effects if the functional currency were changed?

7. After translating Consol-Can's inventory and long-term debt into the parent company's currency (US$), the amounts reported on Consolidated Motor's financial statements on 31 December 20X2 would be *closest* to (in millions):
   A. $71 for inventory and $161 for long-term debt.
   B. $71 for inventory and $166 for long-term debt.
   C. $73 for inventory and $166 for long-term debt.

8. After translating Consol-Can's 31 December 20X2 balance sheet into the parent company's currency (US$), the translated value of retained earnings will be *closest* to:
   A. $41 million.
   B. $44 million.
   C. $46 million.

9. In response to the board's first question, Templeton would *most likely* reply that such a change would be justified if:
   A. the inflation rate in the United States became hyperinflationary.
   B. management wanted to flow more of the gains through net income.
   C. Consol-Can were making autonomous decisions about operations, investing, and financing.

10. In response to the board's second question, Templeton should reply that if the change is made, the consolidated financial statements for Consolidated Motors would begin to recognize:
    A. realized gains and losses on monetary assets and liabilities.
    B. realized gains and losses on non-monetary assets and liabilities.
    C. unrealized gains and losses on non-monetary assets and liabilities.

11. In response to the board's third question, Templeton should note that the change will *most likely* affect:
    A. the cash ratio.
    B. fixed asset turnover.
    C. receivables turnover.

12. In response to the board's fourth question, the balance sheet exposure (in C$ millions) would be *closest* to:
    A. −19.
    B. 148.
    C. 400.

The following information relates to Questions 13–18

Romulus Corp. is a US-based company that prepares its financial statements in accordance with US GAAP. Romulus Corp. has two European subsidiaries: Julius and Augustus. Anthony Marks, CFA, is an analyst trying to forecast Romulus's 20X2 results. Marks has prepared separate forecasts for both Julius and Augustus, as well as for Romulus's other operations (prior to consolidating the results.) He is now considering the impact of currency translation on the results of both the subsidiaries and the parent company's consolidated financials. His research has provided the following insights:

- The results for Julius will be translated into US dollars using the current rate method.
- The results for Augustus will be translated into US dollars using the temporal method.
- Both Julius and Augustus use the FIFO method to account for inventory.
- Julius had year-end 20X1 inventory of €340 million. Marks believes Julius will report €2,300 in sales and €1,400 in cost of sales in 20X2.

Marks also forecasts the 20X2 year-end balance sheet for Julius (Exhibit 1). Data and forecasts related to euro/dollar exchange rates are presented in Exhibit 2.

EXHIBIT 1   Forecasted Balance Sheet Data for Julius, 31 December 20X2 (€ millions)

Cash	50
Accounts receivable	100
Inventory	700
Fixed assets	1,450
Total assets	2,300
Liabilities	700
Common stock	1,500
Retained earnings	100
Total liabilities and shareholder equity	2,300

EXHIBIT 2   Exchange Rates ($/€)

31 December 20X1	1.47
31 December 20X2	1.61
20X2 average	1.54
Rate when fixed assets were acquired	1.25
Rate when 20X1 inventory was acquired	1.39
Rate when 20X2 inventory was acquired	1.49

13. Based on the translation method being used for Julius, the subsidiary is *most likely:*
    A. a sales outlet for Romulus's products.
    B. a self-contained, independent operating entity.
    C. using the US dollar as its functional currency.

14. To account for its foreign operations, Romulus has *most likely* designated the euro as the functional currency for:
    A. Julius only.
    B. Augustus only.
    C. both Julius and Augustus.

15. When Romulus consolidates the results of Julius, any unrealized exchange rate holding gains on monetary assets should be:
    A. reported as part of operating income.
    B. reported as a non-operating item on the income statement.
    C. reported directly to equity as part of the cumulative translation adjustment.

16. When Marks translates his forecasted balance sheet for Julius into US dollars, total assets as of 31 December 20X2 (dollars in millions) will be *closest* to:
    A. $1,429.
    B. $2,392.
    C. $3,703.

17. When Marks converts his forecasted income statement data for Julius into US dollars, the 20X2 gross profit margin will be *closest* to:
    A. 39.1%.
    B. 40.9%.
    C. 44.6%.

18. Relative to the gross margins the subsidiaries report in local currency, Romulus's consolidated gross margin *most likely*:
    A. will not be distorted by currency translations.
    B. would be distorted if Augustus were using the same translation method as Julius.
    C. will be distorted because of the translation and inventory accounting methods Augustus is using.

The following information relates to Questions 19–24

Redline Products, Inc. is a US-based multinational with subsidiaries around the world. One such subsidiary, Acceletron, operates in Singapore, which has seen mild but not excessive rates of inflation. Acceletron was acquired in 2000 and has never paid a dividend. It records inventory using the FIFO method.

Chief Financial Officer Margot Villiers was asked by Redline's board of directors to explain how the functional currency selection and other accounting choices affect Redline's consolidated financial statements. Villiers gathers Acceletron's financial statements denominated in Singapore dollars (SGD) in Exhibit 1 and the US dollar/Singapore dollar exchange rates in Exhibit 2. She does not intend to identify the functional currency actually in use but rather to use Acceletron as an example of how the choice of functional currency affects the consolidated statements.

EXHIBIT 1   Selected Financial Data for
Acceletron, 31 December 2007 (SGD millions)

Cash	SGD125
Accounts receivable	230
Inventory	500
Fixed assets	1,640
Accumulated depreciation	(205)
Total assets	SGD2,290
Accounts payable	185
Long-term debt	200
Common stock	620
Retained earnings	1,285
Total liabilities and equity	2,290
Total revenues	SGD4,800
Net income	SGD450

EXHIBIT 2   Exchange Rates Applicable to Acceletron

Exchange Rate in Effect at Specific Times	USD per SGD
Rate when first SGD1 billion of fixed assets were acquired	0.568
Rate when remaining SGD640 million of fixed assets were acquired	0.606
Rate when long-term debt was issued	0.588
31 December 2006	0.649
Weighted-average rate when inventory was acquired	0.654
Average rate in 2007	0.662
31 December 2007	0.671

19. Compared with using the Singapore dollar as Acceletron's functional currency for 2007, if the US dollar were the functional currency, it is *most likely* that Redline's consolidated:
   A. inventories will be higher.
   B. receivable turnover will be lower.
   C. fixed asset turnover will be higher.

20. If the US dollar were chosen as the functional currency for Acceletron in 2007, Redline could reduce its balance sheet exposure to exchange rates by:
    A. selling SGD30 million of fixed assets for cash.
    B. issuing SGD30 million of long-term debt to buy fixed assets.
    C. issuing SGD30 million in short-term debt to purchase marketable securities.

21. Redline's consolidated gross profit margin for 2007 would be *highest* if Acceletron accounted for inventory using:
    A. FIFO, and its functional currency were the US dollar.
    B. LIFO, and its functional currency were the US dollar.
    C. FIFO, and its functional currency were the Singapore dollar.

22. If the current rate method is used to translate Acceletron's financial statements into US dollars, Redline's consolidated financial statements will *most likely* include Acceletron's:
    A. USD3,178 million in revenues.
    B. USD118 million in long-term debt.
    C. negative translation adjustment to shareholder equity.

23. If Acceletron's financial statements are translated into US dollars using the temporal method, Redline's consolidated financial statements will *most likely* include Acceletron's:
    A. USD336 million in inventory.
    B. USD956 million in fixed assets.
    C. USD152 million in accounts receivable.

24. When translating Acceletron's financial statements into US dollars, Redline is *least likely* to use an exchange rate of USD per SGD:
    A. 0.671.
    B. 0.588.
    C. 0.654.

CHAPTER 17

EVALUATING QUALITY OF FINANCIAL REPORTS

LEARNING OUTCOMES

After completing this chapter, you will be able to do the following:

- demonstrate the use of a conceptual framework for assessing the quality of a company's financial reports;
- explain potential problems that affect the quality of financial reports;
- describe how to evaluate the quality of a company's financial reports;
- evaluate the quality of a company's financial reports;
- describe the concept of sustainable (persistent) earnings;
- describe indicators of earnings quality;
- explain mean reversion in earnings and how the accruals component of earnings affects the speed of mean reversion;
- evaluate the earnings quality of a company;
- describe indicators of cash flow quality;
- evaluate the cash flow quality of a company;
- describe indicators of balance sheet quality;
- evaluate the balance sheet quality of a company;
- describe sources of information about risk.

SUMMARY OVERVIEW

- The quality of financial reporting can be thought of as spanning a continuum from the highest quality to the lowest.

- Potential problems that affect the quality of financial reporting broadly include revenue and expense recognition on the income statement; classification on the statement of cash flows; and the recognition, classification, and measurement of assets and liabilities on the balance sheet.
- Typical steps involved in evaluating financial reporting quality include an understanding of the company's business and industry in which the company is operating; comparison of the financial statements in the current period and the previous period to identify any significant differences in line items; an evaluation of the company's accounting policies, especially any unusual revenue and expense recognition compared with those of other companies in the same industry; financial ratio analysis; examination of the statement of cash flows with particular focus on differences between net income and operating cash flows; perusal of risk disclosures; and review of management compensation and insider transactions.
- High-quality earnings increase the value of the company more than low-quality earnings, and the term "high-quality earnings" assumes that reporting quality is high.
- Low-quality earnings are insufficient to cover the company's cost of capital and/or are derived from non-recurring, one-off activities. In addition, the term "low-quality earnings" can be used when the reported information does not provide a useful indication of the company's performance.
- Various alternatives have been used as indicators of earnings quality: recurring earnings, earnings persistence and related measures of accruals, beating benchmarks, and after-the-fact confirmations of poor-quality earnings, such as enforcement actions and restatements.
- Earnings that have a significant accrual component are less persistent and thus may revert to the mean more quickly.
- A company that consistently reports earnings that exactly meet or only narrowly beat benchmarks can raise questions about its earnings quality.
- Cases of accounting malfeasance have commonly involved issues with revenue recognition, such as premature recognition of revenues or the recognition of fraudulent revenues.
- Cases of accounting malfeasance have involved misrepresentation of expenditures as assets rather than as expenses or misrepresentation of the timing or amount of expenses.
- Bankruptcy prediction models, used in assessing financial results quality, quantify the likelihood that a company will default on its debt and/or declare bankruptcy.
- Similar to the term "earnings quality," when reported cash flows are described as being high quality, it means that the company's underlying economic performance was satisfactory in terms of increasing the value of the firm, and it also implies that the company had high reporting quality (i.e., that the information calculated and disclosed by the company was a good reflection of economic reality). Cash flow can be described as "low quality" either because the reported information properly represents genuinely bad economic performance or because the reported information misrepresents economic reality.
- For the balance sheet, high financial *reporting* quality is indicated by completeness, unbiased measurement, and clear presentation.
- A balance sheet with significant amounts of off-balance-sheet debt would lack the completeness aspect of financial reporting quality.
- Unbiased measurement is a particularly important aspect of financial reporting quality for assets and liabilities for which valuation is subjective.
- A company's financial statements can provide useful indicators of financial or operating risk.
- The management commentary (also referred to as the management discussion and analysis, or MD&A) can give users of the financial statements information that is helpful in assessing the company's risk exposures and approaches to managing risk.

- Required disclosures regarding, for example, changes in senior management or inability to make a timely filing of required financial reports can be a warning sign of problems with financial reporting quality.
- The financial press can be a useful source of information about risk when, for example, a financial reporter uncovers financial reporting issues that had not previously been recognized. An analyst should undertake additional investigation of any issue identified.

PROBLEMS

The following information relates to Questions 1 through 4

Mike Martinez is an equity analyst who has been asked to analyze Stellar, Inc. by his supervisor, Dominic Anderson. Stellar exhibited strong earnings growth last year; however, Anderson is skeptical about the sustainability of the company's earnings. He wants Martinez to focus on Stellar's financial reporting quality and earnings quality.

After conducting a thorough review of the company's financial statements, Martinez concludes the following:

Conclusion 1   Although Stellar's financial statements adhere to generally accepted accounting principles (GAAP), Stellar understates earnings in periods when the company is performing well and overstates earnings in periods when the company is struggling.

Conclusion 2   Stellar most likely understated the value of amortizable intangibles when recording the acquisition of Solar, Inc. last year. No goodwill impairment charges have been taken since the acquisition.

Conclusion 3   Over time, the accruals component of Stellar's earnings is large relative to the cash component.

Conclusion 4   Stellar reported an unusually sharp decline in accounts receivable in the current year, and an increase in long-term trade receivables.

1. Based on Martinez's conclusions, Stellar's financial statements are *best* categorized as:
   A. non-GAAP compliant.
   B. GAAP compliant, but with earnings management.
   C. GAAP compliant and decision useful, with sustainable and adequate returns.

2. Based on Conclusion 2, after the acquisition of Solar, Stellar's earnings are *most likely*:
   A. understated.
   B. fairly stated.
   C. overstated.

3. In his follow-up analysis relating to Conclusion 3, Martinez should focus on Stellar's:
   A. total accruals.
   B. discretionary accruals.
   C. non-discretionary accruals.

4. What will be the impact on Stellar in the current year if Martinez's belief in Conclusion 4 is correct? Compared with the previous year, Stellar's:
   A. current ratio will increase.
   B. days sales outstanding (DSO) will decrease.
   C. accounts receivable turnover will decrease.

18

INTEGRATION OF FINANCIAL STATEMENT ANALYSIS TECHNIQUES

LEARNING OUTCOMES

After completing this chapter, you will be able to do the following:

- demonstrate the use of a framework for the analysis of financial statements, given a particular problem, question, or purpose (e.g., valuing equity based on comparables, critiquing a credit rating, obtaining a comprehensive picture of financial leverage, evaluating the perspectives given in management's discussion of financial results);
- identify financial reporting choices and biases that affect the quality and comparability of companies' financial statements, and explain how such biases may affect financial decisions;
- evaluate the quality of a company's financial data, and recommend appropriate adjustments to improve quality and comparability with similar companies, including adjustments for differences in accounting standards, methods, and assumptions;
- evaluate how a given change in accounting standards, methods, or assumptions affects financial statements and ratios;
- analyze and interpret how balance sheet modifications, earnings normalization, and cash flow statement related modifications affect a company's financial statements, financial ratios, and overall financial condition.

SUMMARY OVERVIEW

The three case studies demonstrate the use of financial analysis in decision making. Each case is set in a different type of industry: manufacturing, service, and financial service. The different focus, purpose, and context for each analysis result in different techniques and tools being applied to the analysis. However, each case demonstrates the use of a common financial state-ment analysis framework. In each case, an economic decision is arrived at; this is consistent with the primary reason for performing financial analysis: to facilitate an economic decision.

PROBLEMS

The following information relates to Questions 1–8

Sergei Leenid, CFA, is a long-only fixed income portfolio manager for the Parliament Funds. He has developed a quantitative model, based on financial statement data, to predict changes in the credit ratings assigned to corporate bond issues. Before applying the model, Leenid first performs a screening process to exclude bonds that fail to meet certain criteria relative to their credit rating. Existing holdings that fail to pass the initial screen are individually reviewed for potential disposition. Bonds that pass the screening process are evaluated using the quantita-tive model to identify potential rating changes.

Leenid is concerned that a pending change in accounting rules could affect the results of the initial screening process. One current screen excludes bonds when the financial leverage ratio (equity multiplier) exceeds a given level and/or the interest coverage ratio falls below a given level for a given bond rating. For example, any "A" rated bond of a company with a fi-nancial leverage ratio exceeding 2.0 or an interest coverage ratio below 6.0 would fail the initial screening. The failing bonds are eliminated from further analysis using the quantitative model.

The new accounting rule would require substantially all leases to be capitalized on a com-pany's balance sheets. To test whether the change in accounting rules will affect the output of the screening process, Leenid collects a random sample of "A" rated bonds issued by compa-nies in the retail industry, which he believes will be among the industries most affected by the change.

Two of the companies, Silk Road Stores and Colorful Concepts, recently issued bonds with similar terms and interest rates. Leenid decides to thoroughly analyze the potential effects of the change on these two companies and begins by gathering information from their most recent annual financial statements (Exhibit 1).

After examining lease disclosures, Leenid estimates the average lease term for each company at 8 years with a fairly consistent lease expense over that time. He believes the leases should be capitalized using 6.5 percent, the rate at which both companies recently issued bonds.

EXHIBIT 1   Selected Financial Data for Silk Road Stores and Colorful Concepts

	Silk Road	Colorful Concepts
Revenue	3,945	7,049
EBIT	318	865
Interest expense	21	35
Income taxes	121	302
Net income	176	528
Average total assets	2,075	3,844
Average total equity	1,156	2,562
Lease expense	213	406

While examining the balance sheet for Colorful Concepts, Leenid also discovers that the company has a 204 ending asset balance (188 beginning) for investments in associates, primarily due to its 20 percent interest in the equity of Exotic Imports. Exotic Imports is a specialty retail chain and in the most recent year reported 1,230 in sales, 105 in net income, and had average total assets of 620.

1. If the accounting rules were to change, Silk Road's assets would increase by approximately:
   A. 1,297.
   B. 1,576.
   C. 1,704.

2. If the accounting rules were to change, Silk Road's interest coverage ratio would be *closest* to:
   A. 3.03.
   B. 3.50.
   C. 5.04.

3. If the accounting rules were to change, Silk Road's financial leverage ratio would be *closest* to:
   A. 1.37.
   B. 1.79.
   C. 2.92.

4. Will the change in accounting rules impact the result of the initial screening process for Colorful Concepts?
   A. It passes the screens now, but will not pass if the accounting rules change.
   B. It passes the screens now and will continue to pass if the accounting rules change.
   C. It fails the screens now and will continue to fail if the accounting rules change.

5. Based on Leenid's analysis of the results of the initial screening, relative to Colorful Concepts the bond rating of Silk Road should be:
   A. lower.
   B. higher.
   C. the same.

6. Ignoring the potential impact of any accounting change and excluding the investment in associates, the net profit margin for Colorful Concepts would be *closest* to:
   A. 6.0%.
   B. 7.2%.
   C. 7.5%.

7. Ignoring the impact of any accounting change, the asset turnover ratio for Colorful Concepts excluding the investments in associates would:
   A. stay the same.
   B. increase by 0.10.
   C. decrease by 0.10.

8. Excluding the investments in associates would result in the interest coverage ratio for Colorful Concepts being:
   A. lower.
   B. higher.
   C. the same.

The following information relates to Questions 9–15

Quentin Abay, CFA, is an analyst for a private equity firm interested in purchasing Bickchip Enterprises, a conglomerate. His first task is to determine the trends in ROE and the main drivers of the trends using DuPont analysis. To do so he gathers the data in Exhibit 1.

EXHIBIT 1   Selected Financial Data for Bickchip Enterprises (€ Thousands)

	2009	2008	2007
Revenue	72,448	66,487	55,781
Earnings before interest and tax	6,270	4,710	3,609
Earnings before tax	5,101	4,114	3,168
Net income	4,038	3,345	2,576
Asset turnover	0.79	0.76	0.68
Assets/Equity	3.09	3.38	3.43

After conducting the DuPont analysis, Abay believes that his firm could increase the ROE without operational changes. Further, Abay thinks that ROE could improve if the company divested segments that were generating the lowest returns on capital employed (total assets less non-interest-bearing liabilities). Segment EBIT margins in 2009 were 11 percent for Automation Equipment, 5 percent for Power and Industrial, and 8 percent for Medical Equipment. Other relevant segment information is presented in Exhibit 2.

EXHIBIT 2   Segment Data for Bickchip Enterprises (€ Thousands)

Operating Segments	Capital Employed			Capital Expenditures (Excluding Acquisitions)		
	2009	2008	2007	2009	2008	2007
Automation Equipment	10,705	6,384	5,647	700	743	616
Power and Industrial	15,805	13,195	12,100	900	849	634
Medical Equipment	22,870	22,985	22,587	908	824	749
	49,380	42,564	40,334	2,508	2,416	1,999

Abay is also concerned with earnings quality, so he intends to calculate Bickchip's cash-flow-based accruals ratio and the ratio of operating cash flow before interest and taxes to operating income. To do so, he prepares the information in Exhibit 3.

EXHIBIT 3   Earnings Quality Data for Bickchip Enterprises (€ Thousands)

	2009	2008	2007
Net income	4,038	3,345	2,576
Net cash flow provided by (used in) operating activity[a]	9,822	5,003	3,198
Net cash flow provided by (used in) investing activity	(10,068)	(4,315)	(5,052)

	2009	2008	2007
Net cash flow provided by (used in) financing activity[b]	(5,792)	1,540	(2,241)
Average net operating assets	43,192	45,373	40,421
[a] includes cash paid for taxes of:	(1,930)	(1,191)	(1,093)
[b] includes cash paid for interest of:	(1,169)	(596)	(441)

9. Over the three-year period presented in Exhibit 1, Bickchip's return on equity is *best* described as:
   A. stable.
   ✓ B. trending lower.
   C. trending higher.

10. Based on the DuPont analysis, Abay's belief regarding ROE is *most likely* based on:
    A. leverage.
    ✓ B. profit margins.
    C. asset turnover.

11. Based on Abay's criteria, the business segment *best* suited for divestiture is:
    ✓ A. medical equipment.
    B. power and industrial.
    C. automation equipment.

12. Bickchip's cash-flow-based accruals ratio in 2009 is *closest* to:
    A. 9.9%.
    B. 13.4%.
    C. 23.3%.

13. The cash-flow-based accruals ratios from 2007 to 2009 indicate:
    A. improving earnings quality.
    B. deteriorating earnings quality.
    C. no change in earnings quality.

14. The ratio of operating cash flow before interest and taxes to operating income for Bickchip for 2009 is *closest* to:
    A. 1.6.
    B. 1.9.
    C. 2.1.

15. Based on the ratios for operating cash flow before interest and taxes to operating income, Abay should conclude that:
    A. Bickchip's earnings are backed by cash flow.
    B. Bickchip's earnings are not backed by cash flow.
    C. Abay can draw no conclusion due to the changes in the ratios over time.

The following information relates to Questions 16–21

Michael Wetstone is an equity analyst covering the software industry for a public pension fund. Prior to comparing the financial results of Software Services Inc. and PDQ GmbH, Wetstone discovers the need to make adjustments to their respective financial statements. The issues preventing comparability, using the financial statements as reported, are the sale of receivables and the impact of minority interests.

Software Services sold $267.5 million of finance receivables to a special purpose entity. PDQ does not securitize finance receivables. An abbreviated balance sheet for Software Services is presented in Exhibit 1.

EXHIBIT 1   Abbreviated Balance Sheet for Software Services ($ 000)

Year Ending:	31 December 2009
Total current assets	1,412,900
Total assets	3,610,600
Total current liabilities	1,276,300
Total liabilities	2,634,100
Total equity	976,500

A significant portion of PDQ's net income is explained by its 20 percent minority interest in Astana Systems. Wetstone collects certain data (Exhibit 2) related to both PDQ and Astana in order to estimate the financials of PDQ on a stand-alone basis.

EXHIBIT 2   Selected Financial Data Related to PDQ and Astana Systems

	PDQ (€ in 000)	Astana ($ in 000)
Earnings before tax (2009)	41,730	15,300
Income taxes (2009)	13,562	5,355
Net income (2009)	28,168	9,945
Market capitalization (recent)	563,355	298,350
Average $/€ exchange rate in 2009	1.55	
Current $/€ exchange rate	1.62	

16. Compared to holding securitized finance receivables on the balance sheet, treating them as sold had the effect of reducing Software Services' reported financial leverage by:
    A. 6.8%.
    B. 7.4%.
    C. 9.2%.

17. Had the securitized finance receivables been held on the balance sheet, Software Services' ratio of liabilities to total capital would have been *closest* to:
    A. 73.0%.
    B. 74.8%.
    C. 80.4%.

18. How much of PDQ's value can be explained by its equity stake in Astana?
    A. 6.5%.
    B. 10.6%.
    C. 20.0%.

19. On a "solo" basis, PDQ's P/E ratio is *closest* to:
    A. 19.6.
    B. 21.0.
    C. 24.5.

20. The adjusted financial statements were created during which phase of the financial analysis process?
    A. Data collection.
    B. Data processing.
    C. Data interpretation.

21. The estimate of PDQ's solo value is crude because of:
    A. the potential differences in accounting standards used by PDQ and Astana.
    B. the differing risk characteristics of PDQ and Astana.
    C. differences in liquidity and market efficiency where PDQ and Astana trade.

SOLUTIONS

CHAPTER 1

FINANCIAL STATEMENT ANALYSIS: AN INTRODUCTION

SOLUTIONS

1. B is correct. This is the role of financial reporting. The role of financial statement analysis is to evaluate the financial reports.

2. A is correct. The balance sheet portrays the current financial position. The income statement and statement of cash flows present different aspects of performance.

3. B is correct. Profitability is the performance aspect measured by the income statement. The balance sheet portrays the current financial position. The statement of cash flows presents a different aspect of performance.

4. C is correct. The notes disclose choices in accounting policies, methods, and estimates.

5. A is correct. Information about management and director compensation is not found in the auditor's report. Disclosure of management compensation is required in the proxy statement, and some aspects of management compensation are disclosed in the notes to the financial statements.

6. B is correct. These are components of management commentary.

7. C is correct. An unqualified opinion is a "clean" opinion and indicates that the financial statements present the company's performance and financial position fairly in accordance with a specified set of accounting standards.

8. C is correct. Ratios are an output of the process data step but are an input into the analyze/interpret data step.

CHAPTER 2

FINANCIAL
REPORTING MECHANICS

SOLUTIONS

1. C is correct. Sales of products, a primary business activity, are classified as an operating activity. Issuance of debt would be a financing activity. Acquisition of a competitor and the sale of surplus equipment would both be classified as investing activities.

2. A is correct. Issuance of debt would be classified as a financing activity. B is incorrect because payment of income taxes would be classified as an operating activity. C is incorrect because investments in common stock would be generally classified as investing activities.

3. A is correct. An asset is an economic resource of an entity that will either be converted into cash or consumed.

4. C is correct. Owners' equity is a residual claim on the resources of a business.

5. A is correct. Assets must equal liabilities plus owners' equity and, therefore, €2,000 = €1,200 + Owners' equity. Owners' equity must be €800.

6. B is correct.

Beginning retained earnings	$1,400
+ Net income	200
– Distributions to owners	(100)
= Ending retained earnings	$1,500

7. C is correct.

Assets = Liabilities + Contributed capital + Beginning retained earnings − Distributions to owners + Revenues − Expenses

Liabilities	$1,000
+ Contributed capital	500
+ Beginning retained earnings	600
− Distributions to owners	(0)
+ Revenues	5,000
− Expenses	(4,300)
= Assets	$2,800

8. C is correct. This is a contribution of capital by the owners. Assets would increase by $500,000 and contributed capital would increase by $500,000, maintaining the balance of the accounting equation.

9. A is correct. The payment of January rent represents prepaid rent (an asset), which will be adjusted at the end of January to record rent expense. Cash (an asset) decreases by $12,000. Deposits (an asset) increase by $4,000. Prepaid rent (an asset) increases by $8,000. There is no net change in assets.

10. B is correct. The sale of products without receipt of cash results in an increase in accounts receivable (an asset) of €10,000. The balance in inventory (an asset) decreases by €8,000. The net increase in assets is €2,000. This would be balanced by an increase in revenue of €10,000 and an increase in expenses (costs of goods sold) of €8,000.

11. C is correct. The receipt of cash in advance of delivering goods or services results in unearned revenue, which is a liability. The company has an obligation to deliver $30,000 in goods in the future. This balances the increase in cash (an asset) of $30,000.

12. B is correct. Depreciation is an expense and increases accumulated depreciation. Accumulated depreciation is a contra account which reduces property, plant, and equipment (an asset) by €250,000. Assets decrease by €250,000, and expenses increase by €250,000.

13. A is correct. The balance sheet shows the financial position of a company at a particular point in time. The balance sheet is also known as a "statement of financial position."

14. B is correct. The three sections of the statement of cash flows are operating, investing, and financing activities.

15. C is correct. Cash received prior to revenue recognition increases cash and deferred or unearned revenue. This is a liability until the company provides the promised goods or services.

16. A is correct. When cash is to be received after revenue has been recognized but no billing has actually occurred, an unbilled (accrued) revenue is recorded. Such accruals would usually occur when an accounting period ends prior to a company billing its customer. This type of accrual can be contrasted with a simple credit sale, which is reflected as an increase in revenue and an increase in accounts receivable. No accrual is necessary.

17. B is correct. Payment of expenses in advance is called a prepaid expense which is classified as an asset.

18. C is correct. When an expense is incurred and no cash has been paid, expenses are increased and a liability ("accrued expense") is established for the same amount.

19. B is correct. The general ledger is the collection of all business transactions sorted by account in an accounting system. The general journal is the collection of all business activities sorted by date.

20. C is correct. In order to balance the accounting equation, the company would either need to increase assets or decrease liabilities. Creating a fictitious asset would be one way of attempting to cover up the fraud.

CHAPTER 3

FINANCIAL REPORTING STANDARDS

SOLUTIONS

1. C is correct. Financial statements provide information, including information about the entity's financial position, performance, and changes in financial position, to users. They do not typically provide information about users.

2. B is correct. The IASB is currently charged with developing International Financial Reporting Standards.

3. B is correct. The FASB is responsible for the Accounting Standards Codification™, the single source of non-governmental authoritative US generally accepted accounting principles.

4. B is correct. Accounting standards boards should be guided by a well articulated framework. They should be independent; and while they consider input from stakeholders, the process should not be compromised by pressure from external forces, including political pressure. Accounting standards boards should have adequate resources.

5. C is correct. A core objective of IOSCO is to ensure that markets are fair, efficient, and transparent. The other core objectives are to reduce, not eliminate, systematic risk and to protect investors, not all users of financial statements.

6. A is correct. Accuracy is not an enhancing qualitative characteristic. Faithful representation, not accuracy, is a fundamental qualitative characteristic.

7. A is correct. Understandability is an enhancing qualitative characteristic of financial information—not a constraint.

8. C is correct. The *Conceptual Framework (2010)* identifies two important underlying assumptions of financial statements: accrual basis and going concern. Going concern is the

assumption that the entity will continue to operate for the foreseeable future. Enterprises with the intent to liquidate or materially curtail operations would require different information for a fair presentation.

9. B is correct. Accrual basis reflects the effects of transactions and other events being recognized when they occur, not when the cash flows. These effects are recorded and reported in the financial statements of the periods to which they relate.

10. C is correct. The fundamental qualitative characteristic of faithful representation is contributed to by completeness, neutrality, and freedom from error.

11. B is correct. Historical cost is the consideration paid to acquire an asset.

12. C is correct. The amount that would be received in an orderly disposal is realizable value.

13. B is correct. There is no statement of changes in income. Under IAS No. 1, a complete set of financial statements includes a statement of financial position, a statement of comprehensive income, a statement of changes in equity, a statement of cash flows, and notes comprising a summary of significant accounting policies and other explanatory information.

14. B is correct. The elements of financial statements related to the measure of performance are income and expenses.

15. A is correct. The elements of financial statements related to the measurement of financial position are assets, liabilities, and equity.

16. A is correct. Timeliness is not a characteristic of a coherent financial reporting framework. Consistency, transparency, and comprehensiveness are characteristics of a coherent financial reporting framework.

17. B is correct. Rules-based, principles-based, and objectives-oriented approaches are recognized approaches to standard-setting.

18. A is correct. A discussion of the impact would be the most meaningful, although B would also be useful.

CHAPTER 4

UNDERSTANDING INCOME STATEMENTS

SOLUTIONS

1. C is correct. IAS No. 1 states that expenses may be categorized by either nature or function.

2. C is correct. Cost of goods sold is a classification by function. The other two expenses represent classifications by nature.

3. C is correct. Gross margin is revenue minus cost of goods sold. Answer A represents net income and B represents operating income.

4. B is correct. Under IFRS, income includes increases in economic benefits from increases in assets, enhancement of assets, and decreases in liabilities.

5. B is correct. Net revenue is revenue for goods sold during the period less any returns and allowances, or $1,000,000 minus $100,000 = $900,000.

6. C is correct. The preferred method is the percentage-of-completion method. The completed contract method should be used under US GAAP only when the outcome cannot be measured reliably. A method similar to, but not referred to as, the cost recovery method is used under IFRS when the outcome cannot be measured reliably.

7. A is correct. Under the completed contract method, no revenue would be reported until the project is completed.

8. A is correct. The installment method apportions the cash receipt between cost recovered and profit using the ratio of profit to sales value (i.e., $3,000,000 ÷ $5,000,000 = 60 percent). Argo will, therefore, recognize $600,000 in profit for 2009 ($1,000,000 cash received × 60 percent).

9. A is correct. Under the cost recovery method, the company would not recognize any profit until the cash amounts paid by the buyer exceeded Argo's cost of $2,000,000.

10. C is correct. Revenue for barter transactions should be measured based on the fair value of revenue from similar non-barter transactions with unrelated parties.

11. A is correct. Apex is not the owner of the goods and should only report its net commission as revenue.

12. B is correct. Under the first in, first out (FIFO) method, the first 10,000 units sold came from the October purchases at £10, and the next 2,000 units sold came from the November purchases at £11.

13. C is correct. Under the weighted average cost method:

October purchases	10,000 units	$100,000
November purchases	5,000 units	$55,000
Total	15,000 units	$155,000

$155,000/15,000 units = $10.3333 × 12,000 units = $124,000.

14. B is correct. The last in, first out (LIFO) method is not permitted under IFRS. The other two methods are permitted.

15. A is correct. Straight-line depreciation would be ($600,000 − $50,000)/10, or $55,000.

16. C is correct. Double-declining balance depreciation would be $600,000 × 20 percent (twice the straight-line rate). The residual value is not subtracted from the initial book value to calculate depreciation. However, the book value (carrying amount) of the asset will not be reduced below the estimated residual value.

17. C is correct. This would result in the highest amount of depreciation in the first year and hence the lowest amount of net income relative to the other choices.

18. B is correct. A fire may be infrequent, but it would still be part of continuing operations. IFRS do not permit classification of an item as extraordinary. Discontinued operations relate to a decision to dispose of an operating division.

19. C is correct. The weighted average number of shares outstanding for 2009 is 1,050,000. Basic earnings per share would be $1,000,000 divided by 1,050,000, or $0.95.

20. A is correct. With stock options, the treasury stock method must be used. Under that method, the company would receive $100,000 (10,000 × $10) and would repurchase 6,667 shares ($100,000/$15). The shares for the denominator would be:

Shares outstanding	1,000,000
Options exercises	10,000
Treasury shares purchased	(6,667)
Denominator	1,003,333

CHAPTER 5

UNDERSTANDING BALANCE SHEETS

SOLUTIONS

1. B is correct. Assets are resources controlled by a company as a result of past events.

2. A is correct. Assets = Liabilities + Equity and, therefore, Assets − Liabilities = Equity.

3. A is correct. A classified balance sheet is one that classifies assets and liabilities as current or non-current and provides a subtotal for current assets and current liabilities. A liquidity-based balance sheet broadly presents assets and liabilities in order of liquidity.

4. B is correct. Goodwill is a long-term asset, and the others are all current assets.

5. A is correct. Current liabilities are those liabilities, including debt, due within one year. Preferred refers to a class of stock. Convertible refers to a feature of bonds (or preferred stock) allowing the holder to convert the instrument into common stock.

6. B is correct. The cash received from customers represents an asset. The obligation to provide a product in the future is a liability called "unearned income" or "unearned revenue." As the product is delivered, revenue will be recognized and the liability will be reduced.

7. C is correct. Under IFRS, inventories are carried at historical cost, unless net realizable value of the inventory is less. Under US GAAP, inventories are carried at the lower of cost or market.

8. C is correct. Paying rent in advance will reduce cash and increase prepaid expenses, both of which are assets.

9. C is correct. Accrued liabilities are expenses that have been reported on a company's income statement but have not yet been paid.

10. A is correct. Initially, goodwill is measured as the difference between the purchase price paid for an acquisition and the fair value of the acquired, not acquiring, company's net assets (identifiable assets less liabilities).

11. C is correct. Impairment write-downs reduce equity in the denominator of the debt-to-equity ratio but do not affect debt, so the debt-to-equity ratio is expected to increase. Impairment write-downs reduce total assets but do not affect revenue. Thus, total asset turnover is expected to increase.

12. B is correct. For financial assets classified as trading securities, unrealized gains and losses are reported on the income statement and flow to shareholders' equity as part of retained earnings.

13. C is correct. For financial assets classified as available for sale, unrealized gains and losses are not recorded on the income statement and instead are part of *other* comprehensive income. Accumulated other comprehensive income is a component of shareholders' equity

14. A is correct. Financial assets classified as held to maturity are measured at amortised cost. Gains and losses are recognized only when realized.

15. B is correct. The non-controlling interest in consolidated subsidiaries is shown separately as part of shareholders' equity.

16. C is correct. The item "retained earnings" is a component of shareholders' equity.

17. B is correct. Share repurchases reduce the company's cash (an asset). Shareholders' equity is reduced because there are fewer shares outstanding and treasury stock is an offset to owners' equity.

18. B is correct. Common-size analysis (as presented in the reading) provides information about composition of the balance sheet and changes over time. As a result, it can provide information about an increase or decrease in a company's financial leverage.

19. A is correct. The current ratio provides a comparison of assets that can be turned into cash relatively quickly and liabilities that must be paid within one year. The other ratios are more suited to longer-term concerns.

20. A is correct. The cash ratio determines how much of a company's near-term obligations can be settled with existing amounts of cash and marketable securities.

21. C is correct. The debt-to-equity ratio, a solvency ratio, is an indicator of financial risk.

22. B is correct. The quick ratio ([Cash + Marketable securities + Receivables] ÷ Current liabilities) is 1.44 ([= 1,884 + 486 + 2,546] ÷ 3,416). Given the placement of other financial assets between cash and receivables, it is reasonable to assume these are highly liquid and are probably marketable securities.

23. C is correct. The financial leverage ratio (Total assets ÷ Total equity) is 1.58 (= 13,374 ÷ 8,491).

CHAPTER 6

UNDERSTANDING CASH FLOW STATEMENTS

SOLUTIONS

1. B is correct. Operating, investing, and financing are the three major classifications of activities in a cash flow statement. Revenues, expenses, and net income are elements of the income statement. Inflows, outflows, and net flows are items of information in the statement of cash flows.

2. B is correct. Purchases and sales of long-term assets are considered investing activities. Note that if the transaction had involved the exchange of a building for other than cash (for example, for another building, common stock of another company, or a long-term note receivable), it would have been considered a significant non-cash activity.

3. C is correct. Payment of dividends is a financing activity under US GAAP. Payment of interest and receipt of dividends are included in operating cash flows under US GAAP. Note that IFRS allow companies to include receipt of interest and dividends as either operating or investing cash flows and to include payment of interest and dividends as either operating or financing cash flows.

4. C is correct. Non-cash transactions, if significant, are reported as supplementary information, not in the investing or financing sections of the cash flow statement.

5. C is correct. Interest expense is always classified as an operating cash flow under US GAAP but may be classified as either an operating or financing cash flow under IFRS.

6. C is correct. Taxes on income are required to be separately disclosed under IFRS and US GAAP. The disclosure may be in the cash flow statement or elsewhere.

7. A is correct. The operating section may be prepared under the indirect method. The other sections are always prepared under the direct method.

8. A is correct. Under the indirect method, the operating section would begin with net income and adjust it to arrive at operating cash flow. The other two items would appear in the operating section under the direct method.

9. A is correct. Revenues of $100 million minus the increase in accounts receivable of $10 million equal $90 million cash received from customers. The increase in accounts receivable means that the company received less in cash than it reported as revenue.

10. C is correct. Cost of goods sold of $80 million plus the increase in inventory of $5 million equals purchases from suppliers of $85 million. The increase in accounts payable of $2 million means that the company paid $83 million in cash ($85 million minus $2 million) to its suppliers.

11. A is correct. Cost of goods sold of $75 million less the decrease in inventory of $6 million equals purchases from suppliers of $69 million. The increase in accounts payable of $2 million means that the company paid $67 million in cash ($69 million minus $2 million).

12. C is correct. Beginning salaries payable of $3 million plus salaries expense of $20 million minus ending salaries payable of $1 million equals $22 million. Alternatively, the expense of $20 million plus the $2 million decrease in salaries payable equals $22 million.

13. C is correct. Cash received from customers = Sales + Decrease in accounts receivable = 254.6 + 4.9 = 259.5. Cash paid to suppliers = Cost of goods sold + Increase in inventory − Increase in accounts payable = 175.9 + 8.8 − 2.6 = 182.1.

14. C is correct. Interest expense of $19 million less the increase in interest payable of $3 million equals interest paid of $16 million. Tax expense of $6 million plus the decrease in taxes payable of $4 million equals taxes paid of $10 million.

15. B is correct. All dollar amounts are in millions. Net income (NI) for 2010 is $35. This amount is the increase in retained earnings, $25, plus the dividends paid, $10. Depreciation of $25 is added back to net income, and the increases in accounts receivable, $5, and in inventory, $3, are subtracted from net income because they are uses of cash. The decrease in accounts payable is also a use of cash and, therefore, a subtraction from net income. Thus, cash flow from operations is $25 + $10 + $25 − $5 − $3 − $7 = $45.

16. A is correct. Selling price (cash inflow) minus book value equals gain or loss on sale; therefore, gain or loss on sale plus book value equals selling price (cash inflow). The amount of loss is given—$2 million. To calculate the book value of the equipment sold, find the historical cost of the equipment and the accumulated depreciation on the equipment.

   - Beginning balance of equipment of $100 million plus equipment purchased of $10 million minus ending balance of equipment of $105 million equals the historical cost of equipment sold, or $5 million.
   - Beginning accumulated depreciation of $40 million plus depreciation expense for the year of $8 million minus ending balance of accumulated depreciation of $46 million equals accumulated depreciation on the equipment sold, or $2 million.
   - Therefore, the book value of the equipment sold was $5 million minus $2 million, or $3 million.
   - Because the loss on the sale of equipment was $2 million, the amount of cash received must have been $1 million.

17. A is correct. The increase of $42 million in common stock and additional paid-in capital indicates that the company issued stock during the year. The increase in retained earnings of $15 million indicates that the company paid $10 million in cash dividends during the year, determined as beginning retained earnings of $100 million plus net income of $25 million minus ending retained earnings of $115 million, which equals $10 million in cash dividends.

18. B is correct. To derive operating cash flow, the company would make the following adjustments to net income: Add depreciation (a non-cash expense) of $2 million; add the decrease in accounts receivable of $3 million; add the increase in accounts payable of $5 million; and subtract the increase in inventory of $4 million. Total additions would be $10 million, and total subtractions would be $4 million, which gives net additions of $6 million.

19. C is correct. An overall assessment of the major sources and uses of cash should be the first step in evaluating a cash flow statement.

20. B is correct. The primary source of cash is operating activities. The primary use of cash is investing activities. Interest received for Telefónica is classified as an investing activity.

21. B is correct. An appropriate method to prepare a common-size cash flow statement is to show each line item on the cash flow statement as a percentage of net revenue. An alternative way to prepare a statement of cash flows is to show each item of cash inflow as a percentage of total inflows and each item of cash outflows as a percentage of total outflows.

22. B is correct. Free cash flow to the firm can be computed as operating cash flows plus after-tax interest expense less capital expenditures.

23. A is correct. This ratio is an interest coverage ratio, measuring a company's ability to meet its interest obligations and indicating a company's solvency. This coverage ratio is based on cash flow information; another common coverage ratio uses a measure based on the income statement (earnings before interest, taxes, depreciation, and amortization).

CHAPTER 7

FINANCIAL ANALYSIS TECHNIQUES

SOLUTIONS

1. C is correct. Cross-sectional analysis involves the comparison of companies with each other for the same time period. Technical analysis uses price and volume data as the basis for investment decisions. Time-series or trend analysis is the comparison of financial data across different time periods.

2. C is correct. Solvency ratios are used to evaluate the ability of a company to meet its long-term obligations. An analyst is more likely to use activity ratios to evaluate how efficiently a company uses its assets. An analyst is more likely to use liquidity ratios to evaluate the ability of a company to meet its short-term obligations.

3. A is correct. The current ratio is a liquidity ratio. It compares the net amount of current assets expected to be converted into cash within the year with liabilities falling due in the same period. A current ratio of 1.0 would indicate that the company would have just enough current assets to pay current liabilities.

4. C is correct. The fixed charge coverage ratio is a coverage ratio that relates known fixed charges or obligations to a measure of operating profit or cash flow generated by the company. Coverage ratios, a category of solvency ratios, measure the ability of a company to cover its payments related to debt and leases.

5. C is correct. The analyst is *unlikely* to reach the conclusion given in Statement C because days of sales outstanding increased from 23 days in FY1 to 25 days in FY2 to 28 days in FY3, indicating that the time required to collect receivables has increased over the period. This is a negative factor for Spherion's liquidity. By contrast, days of inventory on hand dropped over the period FY1 to FY3, a positive for liquidity. The company's increase in days payable, from 35 days to 40 days, shortened its cash conversion cycle, thus also contributing to improved liquidity.

6. A is correct. The company is becoming increasingly less solvent, as evidenced by its debt-to-equity ratio increasing from 0.35 to 0.50 from FY3 to FY5. The amount of a company's debt and equity do not provide direct information about the company's liquidity position.

   Debt to equity:

   FY5: 2,000/4,000 = 0.5000
   FY4: 1,900/4,500 = 0.4222
   FY3: 1,750/5,000 = 0.3500

7. C is correct. The decline in the company's equity indicates that the company may be incurring losses, paying dividends greater than income, or repurchasing shares. Recall that Beginning equity + New shares issuance − Shares repurchased + Comprehensive income − Dividends = Ending equity. The book value of a company's equity is not affected by changes in the market value of its common stock. An increased amount of lending does not necessarily indicate that lenders view a company as increasingly creditworthy. Creditworthiness is not evaluated based on how much a company has increased its debt but rather on its willingness and ability to pay its obligations. (Its financial strength is indicated by its solvency, liquidity, profitability, efficiency, and other aspects of credit analysis.)

8. C is correct. The company's problems with its inventory management system causing duplicate orders would likely result in a higher amount of inventory and would, therefore, result in a decrease in inventory turnover. A more efficient inventory management system and a write off of inventory at the beginning of the period would both likely decrease the average inventory for the period (the denominator of the inventory turnover ratio), thus increasing the ratio rather than decreasing it.

9. B is correct. A write off of receivables would decrease the average amount of accounts receivable (the denominator of the receivables turnover ratio), thus increasing this ratio. Customers with weaker credit are more likely to make payments more slowly or to pose collection difficulties, which would likely increase the average amount of accounts receivable and thus decrease receivables turnover. Longer payment terms would likely increase the average amount of accounts receivable and thus decrease receivables turnover.

10. A is correct. The average accounts receivable balances (actual and desired) must be calculated to determine the desired change. The average accounts receivable balance can be calculated as an average day's credit sales times the DSO. For the most recent fiscal year, the average accounts receivable balance is $15.62 million [= ($300,000,000/365) × 19]. The desired average accounts receivable balance for the next fiscal year is $16.03 million [= ($390,000,000/365) × 15]. This is an increase of $0.41 million (= 16.03 million − 15.62 million). An alternative approach is to calculate the turnover and divide sales by turnover to determine the average accounts receivable balance. Turnover equals 365 divided by DSO. Turnover is 19.21 (= 365/19) for the most recent fiscal year and is targeted to be 24.33 (= 365/15) for the next fiscal year. The average accounts receivable balances are $15.62 million (= $300,000,000/19.21) and $16.03 million (= $390,000,000/24.33). The change is an increase in receivables of $0.41 million

11. A is correct. Company A's current ratio of 4.0 (= $40,000/$10,000) indicates it is more liquid than Company B, whose current ratio is only 1.2 (= $60,000/$50,000). Company B is more solvent, as indicated by its lower debt-to-equity ratio of 30 percent (= $150,000/$500,000) compared with Company A's debt-to-equity ratio of 200 percent (= $60,000/$30,000).

12. C is correct. The company's efficiency deteriorated, as indicated by the decline in its total asset turnover ratio from 1.11 {= 4,390/[(4,384 + 3,500)/2]} for FY10 to 0.87 {= 11,366/[(12,250 + 13,799)/2]} for FY14. The decline in the total asset turnover ratio resulted from an increase in average total assets from GBP3,942 [= (4,384 + 3,500)/2] for FY10 to GBP13,024.5 for FY14, an increase of 230 percent, compared with an increase in revenue from GBP4,390 in FY10 to GBP11,366 in FY14, an increase of only 159 percent. The current ratio is not an indicator of efficiency.

13. B is correct. Comparing FY14 with FY10, the company's solvency deteriorated, as indicated by a decrease in interest coverage from 10.6 (= 844/80) in FY10 to 8.4 (= 1,579/188) in FY14. The debt-to-asset ratio increased from 0.14 (= 602/4,384) in FY10 to 0.27 (= 3,707/13,799) in FY14. This is also indicative of deteriorating solvency. In isolation, the amount of profits does not provide enough information to assess solvency.

14. C is correct. Comparing FY14 with FY10, the company's liquidity improved, as indicated by an increase in its current ratio from 0.71 [= (316 + 558)/1,223] in FY10 to 0.75 [= (682 + 1,634)/3,108] in FY14. Note, however, comparing only current investments with the level of current liabilities shows a decline in liquidity from 0.26 (= 316/1,223) in FY10 to 0.22 (= 682/3,108) in FY14. Debt-to-assets ratio and interest coverage are measures of solvency not liquidity.

15. B is correct. Comparing FY14 with FY10, the company's profitability deteriorated, as indicated by a decrease in its net profit margin from 11.0 percent (= 484/4,390) to 5.7 percent (= 645/11,366). Debt-to-assets ratio is a measure of solvency not an indicator of profitability. Growth in shareholders' equity, in isolation, does not provide enough information to assess profitability.

16. C is correct. Assuming no changes in other variables, an increase in average assets (an increase in the denominator) would decrease ROA. A decrease in either the effective tax rate or interest expense, assuming no changes in other variables, would increase ROA.

17. C is correct. The company's net profit margin has decreased and its financial leverage has increased. ROA = Net profit margin × Total asset turnover. ROA decreased over the period despite the increase in total asset turnover; therefore, the net profit margin must have decreased. ROE = Return on assets × Financial leverage. ROE increased over the period despite the drop in ROA; therefore, financial leverage must have increased.

18. C is correct. The increase in the average tax rate in FY12, as indicated by the decrease in the value of the tax burden (the tax burden equals one minus the average tax rate), offset the improvement in efficiency indicated by higher asset turnover) leaving ROE unchanged. The EBIT margin, measuring profitability, was unchanged in FY12 and no information is given on liquidity.

19. C is correct. The difference between the two companies' ROE in 2010 is very small and is mainly the result of Company A's increase in its financial leverage, indicated by the increase in its Assets/Equity ratio from 2 to 4. The impact of efficiency on ROE is identical for the two companies, as indicated by both companies' asset turnover ratios of 1.5. Furthermore, if Company A had purchased newer equipment to replace older, depreciated equipment, then the company's asset turnover ratio (computed as sales/assets) would have declined, assuming constant sales. Company A has experienced a significant decline in its operating margin, from 10 percent to 7 percent which, all else equal, would not suggest that it is selling more products with higher profit margins.

20. A is correct. The P/E ratio measures the "multiple" that the stock market places on a company's EPS.

21. B is correct. In general, a creditor would consider a decrease in debt to total assets as positive news. A higher level of debt in a company's capital structure increases the risk of default and will, in general, result in higher borrowing costs for the company to compensate lenders for assuming greater credit risk. A decrease in either interest coverage or return on assets is likely to be considered negative news.

22. B is correct. The results of an analyst's financial analysis are integral to the process of developing forecasts, along with the analysis of other information and judgment of the analysts. Forecasts are not limited to a single point estimate but should involve a range of possibilities.

CHAPTER 8

INVENTORIES

SOLUTIONS

1. C is correct. Transportation costs incurred to ship inventory to customers are an expense and may not be capitalized in inventory. (Transportation costs incurred to bring inventory to the business location can be capitalized in inventory.) Storage costs required as part of production, as well as costs incurred as a result of normal waste of materials, can be capitalized in inventory. (Costs incurred as a result of abnormal waste must be expensed.)

2. B is correct. Inventory expense includes costs of purchase, costs of conversion, and other costs incurred in bringing the inventories to their present location and condition. It does not include storage costs not required as part of production.

3. A is correct. IFRS allow the inventories of producers and dealers of agricultural and forest products, agricultural produce after harvest, and minerals and mineral products to be carried at net realizable value even if above historical cost. (U.S. GAAP treatment is similar.)

4. B is correct. Under IFRS, the reversal of write-downs is required if net realizable value increases. The inventory will be reported on the balance sheet at £1,000,000. The inventory is reported at the lower of cost or net realizable value. Under U.S. GAAP, inventory is carried at the lower of cost or market value. After a write-down, a new cost basis is determined and additional revisions may only reduce the value further. The reversal of write-downs is not permitted.

5. A is correct. IFRS require the reversal of inventory write-downs if net realizable values increase; U.S. GAAP do not permit the reversal of write-downs.

6. B is correct. Cinnamon uses the weighted average cost method, so in 2008, 5,000 units of inventory were 2007 units at €10 each and 50,000 were 2008 purchases at €11. The weighted average cost of inventory during 2008 was thus $(5,000 \times 10) + (50,000 \times 11) = 50,000 + 550,000 = €600,000$, and the weighted average cost was approximately €10.91 = €600,000/55,000. Cost of sales was €10.91 × 45,000, which is approximately €490,950.

7. C is correct. Zimt uses the FIFO method, and thus the first 5,000 units sold in 2008 depleted the 2007 inventory. Of the inventory purchased in 2008, 40,000 units were sold and 10,000 remain, valued at €11 each, for a total of €110,000.

8. A is correct. Zimt uses the FIFO method, so its cost of sales represents units purchased at a (no longer available) lower price. Nutmeg uses the LIFO method, so its cost of sales is approximately equal to the current replacement cost of inventory.

9. B is correct. Nutmeg uses the LIFO method, and thus some of the inventory on the balance sheet was purchased at a (no longer available) lower price. Zimt uses the FIFO method, so the carrying value on the balance sheet represents the most recently purchased units and thus approximates the current replacement cost.

10. B is correct. In a declining price environment, the newest inventory is the lowest-cost inventory. In such circumstances, using the LIFO method (selling the newer, cheaper inventory first) will result in lower cost of sales and higher profit.

11. B is correct. In a rising price environment, inventory balances will be higher for the company using the FIFO method. Accounts payable are based on amounts due to suppliers, not the amounts accrued based on inventory accounting.

12. C is correct. The write-down reduced the value of inventory and increased cost of sales in 2007. The higher numerator and lower denominator mean that the inventory turnover ratio as reported was too high. Gross margin and the current ratio were both too low.

13. A is correct. The reversal of the write-down shifted cost of sales from 2008 to 2007. The 2007 cost of sales was higher because of the write-down, and the 2008 cost of sales was lower because of the reversal of the write-down. As a result, the reported 2008 profits were overstated. Inventory balance in 2008 is the same because the write-down and reversal cancel each other out. Cash flow from operations is not affected by the non-cash write-down, but the higher profits in 2008 likely resulted in higher taxes and thus lower cash flow from operations.

14. B is correct. LIFO will result in lower inventory and higher cost of sales. Gross margin (a profitability ratio) will be lower, the current ratio (a liquidity ratio) will be lower, and inventory turnover (an efficiency ratio) will be higher.

15. A is correct. LIFO will result in lower inventory and higher cost of sales in periods of rising costs compared to FIFO. Consequently, LIFO results in a lower gross profit margin than FIFO.

16. B is correct. The LIFO method increases cost of sales, thus reducing profits and the taxes thereon.

17. A is correct. U.S. GAAP do not permit inventory write-downs to be reversed.

18. C is correct. The storage costs for inventory awaiting shipment to customers are not costs of purchase, costs of conversion, or other costs incurred in bringing the inventories to their present location and condition and are not included in inventory. The storage costs for the chocolate liquor occur during the production process and are thus part of the conversion costs. Excise taxes are part of the purchase cost.

19. C is correct. The carrying amount of inventories under FIFO will more closely reflect current replacement values because inventories are assumed to consist of the most recently purchased items. FIFO is an acceptable, but not preferred, method under IFRS. Weighted average cost, not FIFO, is the cost formula that allocates the same per unit cost to both cost of sales and inventory.

20. B is correct. Inventory turnover = Cost of sales/Average inventory = 41,043/7,569.5 = 5.42. Average inventory is (8,100 + 7,039)/2 = 7,569.5.

21. B is correct. For comparative purposes, the choice of a competitor that reports under IFRS is requested because LIFO is permitted under U.S. GAAP.

22. A is correct. The carrying amount of the ending inventory may differ because the perpetual system will apply LIFO continuously throughout the year, liquidating layers as sales are made. Under the periodic system, the sales will start from the last layer in the year. Under FIFO, the sales will occur from the same layers regardless of whether a perpetual or periodic system is used. Specific identification identifies the actual products sold and remaining in inventory, and there will be no difference under a perpetual or periodic system.

23. B is correct. The cost of sales is closest to CHF 4,550. Under FIFO, the inventory acquired first is sold first. Using Exhibit D, a total of 310 cartons were available for sale (100 + 40 + 70 + 100) and 185 cartons were sold (50 + 100 + 35), leaving 125 in ending inventory. The FIFO cost would be as follows:

$$100 \text{ (beginning inventory)} \times 22 = 2{,}200$$

$$40 \text{ (4 February 2009)} \times 25 = 1{,}000$$

$$45 \text{ (23 July 2009)} \times 30 = 1{,}350$$

$$\text{Cost of sales} = 2{,}200 + 1{,}000 + 1{,}350 = \text{CHF } 4{,}550$$

24. A is correct. Gross profit will most likely increase by CHF 7,775. The net realizable value has increased and now exceeds the cost. The write-down from 2008 can be reversed. The write-down in 2008 was 9,256 [92,560 × (4.05 − 3.95)]. IFRS require the reversal of any write-downs for a subsequent increase in value of inventory previously written down. The reversal is limited to the lower of the subsequent increase or the original write-down. Only 77,750 kilograms remain in inventory; the reversal is 77,750 × (4.05 − 3.95) = 7,775. The amount of any reversal of a write-down is recognized as a reduction in cost of sales. The reversal is limited to the lower of the subsequent increase or the original write-down. The amount of any reversal of a write-down is recognized as a reduction in cost of sales. This reduction results in an increase in gross profit.

25. C is correct. Using the FIFO method to value inventories when prices are rising will allocate more of the cost of goods available for sale to ending inventories (the most recent purchases, which are at higher costs, are assumed to remain in inventory) and less to cost of sales (the oldest purchases, which are at lower costs, are assumed to be sold first).

26. C is correct. Karp's inventory under FIFO equals Karp's inventory under LIFO plus the LIFO reserve. Therefore, as of 31 December 2009, Karp's inventory under FIFO equals:

$$\text{Inventory (FIFO method)} = \text{Inventory (LIFO method)} + \text{LIFO reserve}$$
$$= 620 \text{ million} + 155 \text{ million} = 775 \text{ million}$$

27. B is correct. Karp's cost of goods sold (COGS) under FIFO equals Karp's cost of goods sold under LIFO minus the increase in the LIFO reserve. Therefore, for the year ended 31 December 2009, Karp's cost of goods sold under FIFO equals:

$$\text{COGS (FIFO method)} = \text{COGS (LIFO method)} - \text{Increase in LIFO reserve}$$
$$= 2{,}211 \text{ million} - (155 \text{ million} - 117 \text{ million}) = 2{,}173 \text{ million}$$

28. A is correct. Karp's net income (NI) under FIFO equals Karp's net income under LIFO plus the after-tax increase in the LIFO reserve. For the year ended 31 December 2009, Karp's net income under FIFO equals:

NI (FIFO method) = NI (LIFO method) + Increase in LIFO reserve × (1 − tax rate)
= 247 million + 38 million × (1 − 20%) = 277.4 million

Therefore, the increase in net income is:

Increase in NI = NI (FIFO method) − NI (LIFO method)
= 277 million − 247 million = 30.4 million

29. B is correct. Karp's retained earnings (RE) under FIFO equals Karp's retained earnings under LIFO plus the after-tax LIFO reserve. Therefore, for the year ended 31 December 2009, Karp's retained earnings under FIFO equals:

RE (FIFO method) = RE (LIFO method) + LIFO reserve × (1 − tax rate)
= 787 million + 155 million × (1 − 20%) = 911 million

Therefore, the increase in retained earnings is:

Increase in RE = RE (FIFO method) − RE (LIFO method)
= 911 million − 787 million = 124 million

30. A is correct. The cash ratio (cash and cash equivalents ÷ current liabilities) would be lower because cash would have been less under FIFO. Karp's income before taxes would have been higher under FIFO, and consequently taxes paid by Karp would have also been higher and cash would have been lower. There is no impact on current liabilities. Both Karp's current ratio and gross profit margin would have been higher if FIFO had been used. The current ratio would have been higher because inventory under FIFO increases by a larger amount than the cash decreases for taxes paid. Because the cost of goods sold under FIFO is lower than under LIFO, the gross profit margin would have been higher.

31. B is correct. If Karp had used FIFO instead of LIFO, the debt-to-equity ratio would have decreased. No change in debt would have occurred but shareholders' equity would have increased as a result of higher retained earnings.

32. B is correct. Crux's adjusted inventory turnover ratio must be computed using cost of goods sold (COGS) under FIFO and excluding charges for increases in valuation allowances.

COGS (adjusted) = COGS (LIFO method) − Charges included in cost of goods
sold for inventory write-downs − Change in LIFO reserve
= 3,120 million − 13 million − (55 million − 72 million)
= 3,124 million

Note: Minus the change in LIFO reserve is equivalent to plus the decrease in LIFO reserve.

The adjusted inventory turnover ratio is computed using average inventory under FIFO.

$$\text{Ending Inventory (FIFO)} = \text{Ending Inventory (LIFO)} + \text{LIFO reserve}$$

$$\text{Ending Inventory 2009 (FIFO)} = 480 + 55 = 535$$

$$\text{Ending Inventory 2008 (FIFO)} = 465 + 72 = 537$$

$$\text{Average inventory} = (535 + 537)/2 = 536$$

Therefore, adjusted inventory turnover ratio equals:

$$\text{Inventory turnover ratio} = \text{COGS/Average inventory} = 3{,}124/536 = 5.83$$

33. B is correct. Rolby's adjusted net profit margin must be computed using net income (NI) under FIFO and excluding charges for increases in valuation allowances.

$$\begin{aligned}\text{NI (adjusted)} &= \text{NI (FIFO method)} + \text{Charges, included in cost of goods} \\ &\quad\text{sold for inventory write-downs, after-tax} \\ &= 327 \text{ million} + 15 \text{ million} \times (1 - 30\%) = 337.5 \text{ million}\end{aligned}$$

Therefore, adjusted net profit margin equals:

$$\text{Net profit margin} = \text{NI/Revenues} = 337.5/5{,}442 = 6.20\%$$

34. A is correct. Mikko's adjusted debt-to-equity ratio is lower because the debt (numerator) is unchanged and the adjusted shareholders' equity (denominator) is higher. The adjusted shareholders' equity corresponds to shareholders' equity under FIFO, excluding charges for increases in valuation allowances. Therefore, adjusted shareholders' equity is higher than reported (unadjusted) shareholders' equity.

35. C is correct. Mikko's and Crux's gross margin ratios would better reflect the current gross margin of the industry than Rolby because both use LIFO. LIFO recognizes as cost of goods sold the cost of the most recently purchased units, therefore, it better reflects replacement cost. However, Mikko's gross margin ratio best reflects the current gross margin of the industry because Crux's LIFO reserve is decreasing. This could reflect a LIFO liquidation by Crux which would distort gross profit margin.

36. B is correct. The FIFO method shows a higher gross profit margin than the LIFO method in an inflationary scenario, because FIFO allocates to cost of goods sold the cost of the oldest units available for sale. In an inflationary environment, these units are the ones with the lowest cost.

37. A is correct. An inventory write-down increases cost of sales and reduces profit and reduces the carrying value of inventory and assets. This has a negative effect on profitability and solvency ratios. However, activity ratios appear positively affected by a write down because the asset base, whether total assets or inventory (denominator), is reduced. The numerator, sales, in total asset turnover is unchanged and the numerator, cost of sales, in inventory turnover is increased. Thus, turnover ratios are higher and appear more favorable as a result of the write down.

38. B is correct. Finished goods least accurately reflect currents prices because some of the finished goods are valued under the last-in, first-out (LIFO) basis. The costs of the newest units available for sale are allocated to cost of goods sold, leaving the oldest units (at lower costs) in inventory. ZP values raw materials and work in process using the weighted average cost method. While not fully reflecting current prices, some inflationary effect will be included in the inventory values.

39. C is correct. FIFO inventory = Reported inventory + LIFO reserve = 608,572 + 10,120 = 618,692. The LIFO reserve is disclosed in Note 2 of the notes to consolidated financial statements.

40. A is correct. The SEC does not require companies to use the same inventory valuation method for all inventories, so this is the *least likely* reason to change accounting policies regarding inventory. The SEC is currently evaluating whether all U.S. companies should be required to adopt IFRS. If the SEC requires companies to adopt IFRS, the LIFO method of inventory valuation would no longer be allowed.

41. A is correct. The inventory turnover ratio would be lower. The average inventory would be higher under FIFO and cost of products sold would be lower by the increase in LIFO reserve. LIFO is not permitted under IFRS.

Inventory turnover ratio = Cost of products sold ÷ Average inventory

2009 inventory turnover ratio as reported = 10.63 = 5,822,805/
[(608,572 + 486,465)/2].

2009 inventory turnover ratio adjusted to FIFO as necessary = 10.34 = [5,822,805
− (19,660 − 10,120)]/[(608,572 + 10,120 + 486,465 + 19,660)/2].

42. A is correct. No LIFO liquidation occurred during 2009; the LIFO reserve increased from ¥10,120 million in 2008 to ¥19,660 million in 2009. Management stated in the MD&A that the decrease in inventories reflected the impacts of decreased sales volumes and fluctuations in foreign currency translation rates.

43. C is correct. Finished goods and raw materials inventories are lower in 2009 when compared to 2008. Reduced levels of inventory typically indicate an anticipated business contraction.

44. B is correct. The decrease in LIFO inventory in 2009 would typically indicate that more inventory units were sold than produced or purchased. Accordingly, one would expect a liquidation of some of the older LIFO layers and the LIFO reserve to decrease. In actuality, the LIFO reserve *increased* from ¥10,120 million in 2008 to ¥19,660 million in 2009. This is not to be expected and is likely caused by the increase in prices of raw materials, other production materials, and parts of foreign currencies as noted in the MD&A. An analyst should seek to confirm this explanation.

45. B is correct. If prices have been decreasing, write-downs under FIFO are least likely to have a significant effect because the inventory is valued at closer to the new, lower prices. Typically, inventories valued using LIFO are less likely to incur inventory write-downs than inventories valued using weighted average cost or FIFO. Under LIFO, the *oldest* costs are reflected in the inventory carrying value on the balance sheet. Given increasing inventory costs, the inventory carrying values under the LIFO method are already conservatively presented at the oldest and lowest costs. Thus, it is far less likely that inventory write-downs will occur under LIFO; and if a write-down does occur, it is likely to be of a lesser magnitude.

CHAPTER 9

LONG-LIVED ASSETS

SOLUTIONS

1. B is correct. Only costs necessary for the machine to be ready to use can be capitalized. Therefore, Total capitalized costs = 12,980 + 1,200 + 700 + 100 = $14,980.

2. A is correct. Borrowing costs can be capitalized under IFRS until the tangible asset is ready for use. Also, under IFRS, income earned on temporarily investing the borrowed monies decreases the amount of borrowing costs eligible for capitalization. Therefore, Total capitalized interest = (500 million × 14% × 2 years) − 10 million = 130 million.

3. B is correct. A product patent with a defined expiration date is an intangible asset with a finite useful life. A copyright with no expiration date is an intangible asset with an indefinite useful life. Goodwill is no longer considered an intangible asset under IFRS and is considered to have an indefinite useful life.

4. C is correct. An intangible asset with a finite useful life is amortized, whereas an intangible asset with an indefinite useful life is not.

5. A is correct. If the company uses the straight-line method, the depreciation expense will be one-fifth (20 percent) of the depreciable cost in Year 1. If it uses the units-of-production method, the depreciation expense will be 19 percent (2,000/10,500) of the depreciable cost in Year 1. Therefore, if the company uses the straight-line method, its depreciation expense will be higher and its net income will be lower.

6. C is correct. If Martinez wants to minimize tax payments in the first year of the machine's life, he should use an accelerated method, such as the double-declining balance method.

7. A is correct. Using the straight-line method, depreciation expense amounts to

   Depreciation expense = (1,200,000 − 200,000)/8 years = 125,000.

8. B is correct. Using the units-of-production method, depreciation expense amounts to

   Depreciation expense = (1,200,000 − 200,000) × (135,000/800,000) = 168,750.

9. A is correct. The straight-line method is the method that evenly distributes the cost of an asset over its useful life because amortization is the same amount every year.

10. A is correct. A higher residual value results in a lower total depreciable cost and, therefore, a lower amount of amortization in the first year after acquisition (and every year after that).

11. B is correct. Using the straight-line method, accumulated amortization amounts to

    Accumulated amortization = [(2,300,000 − 500,000)/3 years] × 2 years = 1,200,000.

12. B is correct. Using the units-of-production method, depreciation expense amounts to

    Depreciation expense = 5,800,000 × (20,000/175,000) = 662,857.

13. B is correct. In this case, the value increase brought about by the revaluation should be recorded directly in equity. The reason is that under IFRS, an increase in value brought about by a revaluation can only be recognized as a profit to the extent that it reverses a revaluation decrease of the same asset previously recognized in the income statement.

14. B is correct. The impairment loss equals £3,100,000.

    Impairment = max(Recoverable amount; Value in use) − Net carrying amount
               = max(16,800,000 − 800,000; 14,500,000) − 19,100,000 = −3,100,000.

15. B is correct. The result on the sale of the vehicle equals

    Gain or loss on the sale = Sale proceeds − Carrying amount
                             = Sale proceeds − (Acquisition cost − Accumulated depreciation)
                             = 85,000 − {100,000 − [((100,000 − 10,000)/9 years) × 3 years]}
                             = 15,000.

16. A is correct. Gain or loss on the sale = Sale proceeds − Carrying amount. Rearranging this equation, Sale proceeds = Carrying amount + Gain or loss on sale. Thus, Sale price = (12 million − 2 million) + (−3.2 million) = 6.8 million.

17. B is correct. IFRS do not require acquisition dates to be disclosed.

18. A is correct. IFRS do not require fair value of intangible assets to be disclosed.

19. B is correct. Investment property earns rent. Investment property and property, plant, and equipment are tangible and long-lived.

20. C is correct. When a company uses the fair value model to value investment property, changes in the fair value of the property are reported in the income statement—not in other comprehensive income.

21. A is correct. Investment property earns rent. Inventory is held for resale, and property, plant, and equipment are used in the production of goods and services.

22. C is correct. A company will change from the fair value model to either the cost model or revaluation model when the company transfers investment property to property, plant, and equipment.

23. C is correct. Expensing rather than capitalizing an investment in long-term assets will result in higher expenses and lower net income and net profit margin in the current year. Future years' incomes will not include depreciation expense related to these expenditures. Consequently, year-to-year growth in profitability will be higher. If the expenses had been capitalized, the carrying amount of the assets would have been higher and the 2009 total asset turnover would have been lower.

24. C is correct. In 2010, switching to an accelerated depreciation method would increase depreciation expense and decrease income before taxes, taxes payable, and net income. Cash flow from operating activities would increase because of the resulting tax savings.

25. B is correct. 2009 net income and net profit margin are lower because of the impairment loss. Consequently, net profit margins in subsequent years are likely to be higher. An impairment loss suggests that insufficient depreciation expense was recognized in prior years, and net income was overstated in prior years. The impairment loss is a non-cash item and will not affect operating cash flows.

26. A is correct. The estimated average remaining useful life is 20.75 years.

$$\text{Estimate of remaining useful life} = \text{Net plant and equipment} \div \text{Annual depreciation expense}$$

$$\text{Net plant and equipment} = \text{Gross P\&E} - \text{Accumulated depreciation}$$
$$= €6000 - €1850 = €4150$$

$$\text{Estimate of remaining useful life} = \text{Net P\&E} \div \text{Depreciation expense}$$
$$= €4150 \div €200 = 20.75$$

27. A is correct. When leases are classified as finance leases, the lessee initially reports an asset and liability at a carrying amount equal to the lower of the fair value of the leased asset or the present value of the future lease payments. Under an operating lease, the lessee does not report an asset or liability. Therefore, total asset turnover (Total revenue ÷ Average total assets) would be lower if the leases were classified as finance leases.

28. C is correct. Total liabilities-to-assets would be higher. When leases are classified as finance leases, the lessee initially reports an asset and liability at a carrying amount equal to the lower of the fair value of the leased asset or the present value of the future lease payments. Both the numerator and denominator would increase by an equal amount, but the proportional increase in the numerator is higher and the ratio would be higher. The following exhibit shows what would happen to 2009 total liabilities, assets, and total liabilities-to-assets if €200 million, the fair value of the leased equipment, is added to AMRC's total liabilities and assets. This simple example ignores the impact of accounting for the 2009 lease payment.

	2009 Actual Under Operating Lease	2009 Hypothetical Under Finance Lease
Total liabilities	€2,750	€2,950
Total assets	€5,350	€5,550
Total liabilities-to-assets	51.4%	53.2%

The depreciation and interest expense under a finance lease tends to be higher than the operating lease payment in the early years of the lease. The finance lease would result in lower net income and net profit margin. Long-lived (fixed) assets are higher under a finance lease and fixed asset turnover is lower.

29. C is correct. The decision to capitalize the costs of the new computer system results in higher cash flow from operating activities; the expenditure is reported as an outflow of investing activities. The company allocates the capitalized amount over the asset's useful life as depreciation or amortization expense rather than expensing it in the year of expenditure. Net income and total assets are higher in the current fiscal year.

30. B is correct. Alpha's fixed asset turnover will be lower because the capitalized interest will appear on the balance sheet as part of the asset being constructed. Therefore, fixed assets will be higher and the fixed asset turnover ratio (Total revenue/Average net fixed assets) will be lower than if it had expensed these costs. Capitalized interest appears on the balance sheet as part of the asset being constructed instead of being reported as interest expense in the period incurred. However, the interest coverage ratio should be based on interest payments, not interest expense (Earnings before interest and taxes/Interest payments), and should be unchanged. To provide a true picture of a company's interest coverage, the entire amount of interest expenditure, both the capitalized portion and the expensed portion, should be used in calculating interest coverage ratios.

31. C is correct. The cash flow from operating activities will be lower, not higher, because the full lease payment is treated as an operating cash outflow. With a finance lease, only the portion of the lease payment relating to interest expense potentially reduces operating cash outflows. A company reporting a lease as an operating lease will typically show higher profits in early years, because the lease expense is less than the sum of the interest and depreciation expense. The company reporting the lease as an operating lease will typically report stronger solvency and activity ratios.

32. A is correct. Accelerated depreciation will result in an improving, not declining, net profit margin over time, because the amount of depreciation expense declines each year. Under straight-line depreciation, the amount of depreciation expense will remain the same each year. Under the units-of-production method, the amount of depreciation expense reported each year varies with the number of units produced.

33. B is correct. The estimated average total useful life of a company's assets is calculated by adding the estimates of the average remaining useful life and the average age of the assets. The average age of the assets is estimated by dividing accumulated depreciation by depreciation expense. The average remaining useful life of the asset base is estimated by dividing net property, plant, and equipment by annual depreciation expense.

34. C is correct. The impairment loss is a non-cash charge and will not affect cash flow from operating activities. The debt to total assets and fixed asset turnover ratios will increase, because the impairment loss will reduce the carrying amount of fixed assets and therefore total assets.

35. A is correct. In an asset revaluation, the carrying amount of the assets increases. The increase in the asset's carrying amount bypasses the income statement and is reported as other comprehensive income and appears in equity under the heading of revaluation surplus. Therefore, shareholders' equity will increase but net income will not be affected, so return on equity will decline. Return on assets and debt to capital ratios will also decrease.

CHAPTER 10

NON-CURRENT
(LONG-TERM) LIABILITIES

SOLUTIONS

1. B is correct. The company receives €1 million in cash from investors at the time the bonds are issued, which is recorded as a financing activity.

2. B is correct. The effective interest rate is greater than the coupon rate and the bonds will be issued at a discount.

3. A is correct. Under US GAAP, expenses incurred when issuing bonds are generally recorded as an asset and amortised to the related expense (legal, etc.) over the life of the bonds. Under IFRS, they are included in the measurement of the liability. The related cash flows are financing activities.

4. B is correct. The bonds will be issued at a discount because the market interest rate is higher than the stated rate. Discounting the future payments to their present value indicates that at the time of issue, the company will record £978,938 as both a liability and a cash inflow from financing activities. Interest expense in 2010 is £58,736 (£978,938 times 6.0 percent). During the year, the company will pay cash of £55,000 related to the interest payment, but interest expense on the income statement will also reflect £3,736 related to amortisation of the initial discount (£58,736 interest expense less the £55,000 interest payment). Thus, the value of the liability at 31 December 2010 will reflect the initial value (£978,938) plus the amortised discount (£3,736), for a total of £982,674. The cash outflow of £55,000 may be presented as either an operating or financing activity under IFRS.

5. A is correct. The coupon rate on the bonds is higher than the market rate, which indicates that the bonds will be issued at a premium. Taking the present value of each payment indicates an issue date value of €10,210,618. The interest expense is determined by multiplying the carrying amount at the beginning of the period (€10,210,618) by the market interest rate at the time of issue (6.0 percent) for an interest expense of €612,637. The value after one year will equal the beginning value less the amount of the premium amortised to date,

which is the difference between the amount paid (€650,000) and the expense accrued (€612,637) or €37,363. €10,210,618 − €37,363 = €10,173,255 or €10.17 million.

6. C is correct. A gain of €3.3 million (carrying amount less amount paid) will be reported on the income statement.

7. A is correct. The value of the liability for zero-coupon bonds increases as the discount is amortised over time. Furthermore, the amortised interest will reduce earnings at an increasing rate over time as the value of the liability increases. Higher relative debt and lower relative equity (through retained earnings) will cause the debt-to-equity ratio to increase as the zero-coupon bonds approach maturity.

8. A is correct. When interest rates rise, bonds decline in value. Thus, the carrying amount of the bonds being carried on the balance sheet is higher than the market value. The company could repurchase the bonds for less than the carrying amount, so the economic liabilities are overestimated. Because the bonds are issued at a fixed rate, there is no effect on interest coverage.

9. C is correct. Covenants protect debtholders from excessive risk taking, typically by limiting the issuer's ability to use cash or by limiting the overall levels of debt relative to income and equity. Issuing additional equity would increase the company's ability to meet its obligations, so debtholders would not restrict that ability.

10. B is correct. An operating lease is not recorded on the balance sheet (debt is lower), and lease payments are entirely categorised as rent (interest expense is lower.) Because the rent expense is an operating outflow but principal repayments are financing cash flows, the operating lease will result in lower cash flow from operating activity.

11. B is correct. The lessee will disclose the future obligation by maturity of its operating leases. The future obligations by maturity, leased assets, and lease liabilities will all be shown for finance leases.

12. B is correct. When a lease is classified as an operating lease, the underlying asset remains on the lessor's balance sheet. The lessor will record a depreciation expense that reduces the asset's value over time.

13. A is correct. A sales-type lease treats the lease as a sale of the asset, and revenue is recorded at the time of sale equal to the present value of future lease payments. Under a direct financing lease, only interest income is reported as earned. Under an operating lease, revenue from rent is reported when collected.

14. A is correct. A portion of the payments for capital leases, either direct financing or sales-type, is reported as interest income. With an operating lease, all revenue is recorded as rental revenue.

15. C is correct. The current debt-to-total-capital ratio is $840/($840+$520) = 0.62. To adjust for the lease commitments, an analyst should add $100 to both the numerator and denominator: $940/($940+$520) = 0.64.

16. B is correct. The company will report a net pension obligation of €1 million equal to the pension obligation (€10 million) less the plan assets (€9 million).

CHAPTER 11

FINANCIAL REPORTING QUALITY

SOLUTIONS

1. C is correct. Financial reporting quality pertains to the quality of the information contained in financial reports. High-quality financial reports provide decision-useful information that faithfully represents the economic reality of the company. Low-quality financial reports impede assessment of earnings quality. Financial reporting quality is distinguishable from earnings quality, which pertains to the earnings and cash generated by the company's actual economic activities and the resulting financial condition. Low-quality earnings are not sustainable and decrease company value.

2. B is correct. Financial reporting quality pertains to the quality of the information contained in financial reports. If financial reporting quality is low, the information provided is not useful to assess the company's performance. Financial reporting quality is distinguishable from earnings quality, which pertains to the earnings and cash generated by the company's actual economic activities and the resulting financial condition.

3. B is correct. Earnings quality pertains to the earnings and cash generated by the company's actual economic activities and the resulting financial condition. Low-quality earnings are likely not sustainable over time because the company does not expect to generate the same level of earnings in the future or because earnings will not generate sufficient return on investment to sustain the company in the future. Earnings that are not sustainable decrease company value. Earnings quality is distinguishable from financial reporting quality, which pertains to the quality of the information contained in financial reports.

4. A is correct. Financial reports span a quality continuum from high to low based on decision-usefulness and earnings quality (see Exhibit 2 of the reading). The lowest-quality reports portray fictitious events, which may misrepresent the company's performance and/or obscure fraudulent misappropriation of the company's assets.

5. B is correct. Aggressive accounting choices aim to enhance the company's reported performance by inflating the amount of revenues, earnings, and/or operating cash flow reported in the period. Consequently, the financial performance for the current period would most likely exhibit an upward bias.

6. C is correct. Accounting choices are considered conservative if they decrease the company's reported performance and financial position in the current period. Conservative choices may increase the amount of debt reported on the balance sheet. Conservative accounting choices may decrease the amount of revenues, earnings, and/or operating cash flow reported in the current period and increase those amounts in later periods.

7. A is correct. Managers often have incentives to meet or beat market expectations, particularly if management compensation is linked to increases in stock prices or to reported earnings.

8. C is correct. In a period of strong financial performance, managers may pursue accounting choices that increase the probability of exceeding next period's earnings forecasts. By accelerating expense recognition or delaying revenue recognition, managers may increase earnings in the next period and increase the likelihood of exceeding next period's earnings targets.

9. A is correct. The possibility of bond covenant violations may motivate managers to inflate earnings in the current period. By inflating earnings in the current period, the company may be able to avoid the consequences associated with violating bond covenants.

10. A is correct. Opportunities to issue low quality financial reports include internal conditions such as an ineffective board of directors and external conditions such as accounting standards that provide scope for divergent choices. Pressure to achieve some performance level and corporate concerns about financing in the future are examples of motivations to issue low-quality financial reports. Typically, three conditions exist when low-quality financial reports are issued: opportunity, motivation, and rationalization.

11. C is correct. An audit is intended to provide assurance that the company's financial reports are presented fairly, thus providing discipline regarding financial reporting quality. Regulatory agencies usually require that the financial statements of publicly traded companies be audited by an independent auditor to provide assurance that the financial statements conform to accounting standards. Privately held companies may also choose to obtain audit opinions either voluntarily or because an outside party requires it. An audit is not typically intended to detect fraud. An audit is based on sampling and it is possible that the sample might not reveal misstatements.

12. B is correct. If a company uses a non-GAAP financial measure in an SEC filing, it is required to provide the most directly comparable GAAP measure with equivalent prominence in the filing. In addition, the company is required to provide a reconciliation between the non-GAAP measure and the equivalent GAAP measure. Similarly, IFRS require that any non-IFRS measures included in financial reports must be defined and their potential relevance explained. The non-IFRS measures must be reconciled with IFRS measures.

13. B is correct. If a company wants to increase reported earnings, the company's managers may reduce the allowance for uncollected accounts and uncollected accounts expense reported in the period. Decreasing the useful life of depreciable assets would increase

depreciation expense and decrease earnings in the current period. Classifying a purchase as an expense rather than a capital expenditure would decrease earnings in the current period. The use of accrual accounting may result in estimates included in financial reports, because all facts associated with events may not be known at the time of recognition. These estimates can be grounded in reality or can be managed by the company to present a desired financial picture.

14. B is correct. Bias in revenue recognition can lead to manipulation of information presented in financial reports. Addressing the question as to whether revenue is higher or lower than the previous period is not sufficient to determine if there is bias in revenue recognition. Additional analytical procedures must be performed to provide warning signals of accounting malfeasance. Barter transactions are difficult to value properly and may result in bias in revenue recognition. Policies that make it easier to prematurely recognize revenue, such as revenue being recognized before goods are shipped to customers, may be a warning sign of accounting malfeasance.

15. C is correct. If a company's days sales outstanding (DSO) is increasing relative to competitors, this may be a signal that revenues are being recorded prematurely or are even fictitious. There are numerous analytical procedures that can be performed to provide evidence of manipulation of information in financial reporting. These warning signs are often linked to bias associated with revenue recognition and expense recognition policies.

16. B is correct. If the ratio of cash flow to net income for a company is consistently below 1 or has declined repeatedly over time, this may be a signal of manipulation of information in financial reports through aggressive accrual accounting policies. When net income is consistently higher than cash provided by operations, one possible explanation is that the company may be using aggressive accrual accounting policies to shift current expenses to later periods.

CHAPTER 12

FINANCIAL STATEMENT ANALYSIS: APPLICATIONS

SOLUTIONS

1. C is correct. For a large, diversified company, margin changes in different business segments may offset each other. Furthermore, margins are most likely to be stable in mature industries.

2. C is correct. Accounts receivable turnover is equal to 365/19 (collection period in days) = 19.2 for 2003 and needs to equal 365/15 = 24.3 in 2004 for Galambos to meet its goal. Sales/turnover equals the accounts receivable balance. For 2003, $300,000,000/19.2 = $15,625,000, and for 2004, $400,000,000/24.3 = $16,460,905. The difference of $835,905 is the increase in receivables needed for Galambos to achieve its goal.

3. C is correct. Credit analysts consider both business risk and financial risk.

4. A is correct. Requiring that net income be positive would eliminate companies that report a positive return on equity only because both net income and shareholders' equity are negative.

5. B is correct. A lower value of debt/total assets indicates greater financial strength. Requiring that a company's debt/total assets be below a certain cutoff point would allow the analyst to screen out highly leveraged and, therefore, potentially financially weak companies.

6. C is correct. Survivorship bias exists when companies that merge or go bankrupt are dropped from the database and only surviving companies remain. Look-ahead bias involves using updated financial information in back-testing that would not have been available at the time the decision was made. Back-testing involves testing models in prior periods and is not, itself, a bias.

7. C is correct. Financial statements should be adjusted for differences in accounting standards (as well as accounting and operating choices). These adjustments should be made prior to common-size and ratio analysis.

8. C is correct. IFRS makes a distinction between unrealized gains and losses on available-for-sale debt securities that arise as a result of exchange rate movements and requires these changes in value to be recognized in the income statement, whereas US GAAP does not make this distinction.

9. A is correct. LIFO is not permitted under IFRS.

10. C is correct. To convert LIFO inventory to FIFO inventory, the entire LIFO reserve must be added back: $600,000 + $70,000 = $670,000.

11. C is correct. The company made no additions to or deletions from the fixed asset account during the year, so depreciation expense is equal to the difference in accumulated depreciation at the beginning of the year and the end of the year, or $0.4 million. Average age is equal to accumulated depreciation/depreciation expense, or $1.6/$0.4 = 4 years. Average depreciable life is equal to ending gross investment/depreciation expense = $2.8/$0.4 = 7 years.

12. C is correct. Tangible book value removes all intangible assets, including goodwill, from the balance sheet.

13. B is correct. Operating leases can be used as an off-balance-sheet financing technique because neither the asset nor liability appears on the balance sheet. Inventory and capital leases are reported on the balance sheet.

14. C is correct. The present value of future operating lease payments would be added to total assets and total liabilities.

CHAPTER 13

INCOME TAXES

SOLUTIONS

1. C is correct. Because the differences between tax and financial accounting will correct over time, the resulting deferred tax liability, for which the expense was charged to the income statement but the tax authority has not yet been paid, will be a temporary difference. A valuation allowance would only arise if there was doubt over the company's ability to earn sufficient income in the future to require paying the tax.

2. A is correct. The taxes a company must pay in the immediate future are taxes payable.

3. C is correct. Higher reported tax expense relative to taxes paid will increase the deferred tax liability, whereas lower reported tax expense relative to taxes paid increases the deferred tax asset.

4. B is correct. If the liability is expected to reverse (and thus require a cash tax payment) the deferred tax represents a future liability.

5. A is correct. If the liability will not reverse, there will be no required tax payment in the future and the "liability" should be treated as equity.

6. C is correct. The deferred tax liability should be excluded from both debt and equity when both the amounts and timing of tax payments resulting from the reversals of temporary differences are uncertain.

7. C is correct. Accounting items that are not deductible for tax purposes will not be reversed and thus result in permanent differences.

8. C is correct. Tax credits that directly reduce taxes are a permanent difference, and permanent differences do not give rise to deferred tax.

9. A is correct. The capitalization will result in an asset with a positive tax base and zero carrying value. The amortization means the difference is temporary. Because there is a temporary difference on an asset resulting in a higher tax base than carrying value, a deferred tax asset is created.

10. B is correct. The difference is temporary, and the tax base will be lower (because of more rapid amortization) than the carrying value of the asset. The result will be a deferred tax liability.

11. A is correct. The advances represent a liability for the company. The carrying value of the liability exceeds the tax base (which is now zero). A deferred tax asset arises when the carrying value of a liability exceeds its tax base.

12. B is correct. The income tax provision in 2007 was $54,144, consisting of $58,772 in current income taxes, of which $4,628 were deferred.

13. B is correct. The effective tax rate of 30.1 percent ($56,860/$189,167) was higher than the effective rates in 2005 and 2007.

14. A is correct. In 2007 the effective tax rate on foreign operations was 24.2 percent [($28,140 + $124)/$116,704] and the effective US tax rate was [($30,632 − $4,752)/$88,157] = 29.4 percent. In 2006 the effective tax rate on foreign operations was 26.2 percent and the US rate was 35.9 percent. In 2005 the foreign rate was 24.1 percent and the US rate was 35.5 percent.

15. B is correct. The valuation allowance is taken against deferred tax assets to represent uncertainty that future taxable income will be sufficient to fully utilize the assets. By decreasing the allowance, Zimt is signaling greater likelihood that future earnings will be offset by the deferred tax asset.

16. C is correct. The valuation allowance is taken when the company will "more likely than not" fail to earn sufficient income to offset the deferred tax asset. Because the valuation allowance equals the asset, by extension the company expects *no* taxable income prior to the expiration of the deferred tax assets.

17. A is correct. A lower tax rate would increase net income on the income statement, and because the company has a net deferred tax liability, the net liability position on the balance sheet would also improve (be smaller).

18. C is correct. The reduction in the valuation allowance resulted in a corresponding reduction in the income tax provision.

19. B is correct. The net deferred tax liability was smaller in 2007 than it was in 2006, indicating that in addition to meeting the tax payments provided for in 2007 the company also paid taxes that had been deferred in prior periods.

20. C is correct. The income tax provision at the statutory rate of 34 percent is a benefit of $112,000, suggesting that the pre-tax income was a loss of $112,000/0.34 = ($329,412). The income tax provision was $227,000. ($329,412) − $227,000 = ($556,412).

21. C is correct. Accounting expenses that are not deductible for tax purposes result in a permanent difference, and thus do not give rise to deferred taxes.

22. B is correct. Over the three-year period, changes in the valuation allowance reduced cumulative income taxes by $1,670,000. The reductions to the valuation allowance were a result of the company being "more likely than not" to earn sufficient taxable income to offset the deferred tax assets.

CHAPTER 14

EMPLOYEE COMPENSATION: POST-EMPLOYMENT AND SHARE-BASED

SOLUTIONS

1. B is correct. The £28,879 million year-end benefit obligation represents the defined benefit obligation.

2. C is correct. The net interest expense of £273 million represents the interest cost on the beginning net pension obligation (beginning funded status) using the discount rate that the company uses in estimating the present value of its pension obligations. This is calculated as −£4,984 million times 5.48 percent = −£273 million; this represents an interest expense on the amount that the company essentially owes the pension plan.

3. C is correct. The remeasurement component of periodic pension cost includes both actuarial gains and losses on the pension obligation and net return on plan assets. Because Kensington does not have any actuarial gains and losses on the pension obligation, the remeasurement component includes only net return on plan assets. In practice, actuarial gains and losses are rarely equal to zero. The net return on plan assets is equal to actual returns minus beginning plan assets times the discount rate, or £1,302 million − (£23,432 million × 0.0548) = £18 million.

4. A is correct. The actual return on plan assets was 1,302/23,432 = 0.0556, or 5.56 percent. The rate of return included in the interest income/expense is the discount rate, which is given in this example as 5.48 percent.

   The rate of 1.17 percent, calculated as the net interest income divided by beginning plan assets, is not used in pension cost calculations.

5. C is correct. Under IFRS, the component of periodic pension cost that is shown in OCI rather than P&L is remeasurments.

6. A is correct. The relation between the periodic pension cost and the plan's funded status can be expressed as Periodic pension cost = Ending funded status − Employer contributions − Beginning funded status.

7. B is correct. Kensington's periodic pension cost was £483. The company's contributions to the plan were £693. The £210 difference between these two numbers can be viewed as a reduction of the overall pension obligation. To adjust the statement of cash flows to reflect this view, an analyst would reclassify the £210 million (excluding income tax effects) as an outflow related to financing activities rather than operating activities.

8. C is correct. The retirement benefits paid during the year were closest to 4,000. The beginning obligation plus current and past service costs plus interest expense plus increase in obligation due to actuarial loss less ending obligation equals benefits paid (= 42,000 + 200 + 120 + (42,000 × 0.07) + 460 − 41,720 = 4,000). Beginning plan assets plus contributions plus actual return on plan assets less ending plan assets equals benefits paid (= 39,000 + 1,000 + 2,700 − 38,700 = 4,000).

9. B is correct. The total periodic pension cost is the change in the net pension liability adjusted for the employer's contribution into the plan. The net pension liability increased from 3,000 to 3,020, and the employer's contribution was 1,000. The total periodic pension cost is 1,020. This will be allocated between P&L and OCI.

10. B is correct. Under IFRS, the components of periodic pension cost that would be reported in P&L are the service cost (composed of current service and past service costs) and the net interest expense or income, calculated by multiplying the net pension liability or net pension asset by the discount rate used to measure the pension liability. Here, the service costs are 320 (= 200 + 120) and the net interest expense is 210 [= (42,000 − 39,000) × 7%]. Thus, the total periodic pension cost is equal to 530.

11. A is correct. Under US GAAP—assuming the company chooses not to immediately recognise the actuarial loss and assuming there is no amortisation of past service costs or actuarial gains and losses—the components of periodic pension cost that would be reported in P&L include the current service cost of 200, the interest expense on the pension obligation at the beginning of the period of 2,940 (= 7.0% × 42,000), and the expected return on plan assets, which is a reduction of the cost of 3,120 (= 8.0% × 39,000). Summing these three components gives 20.

12. B is correct. The component of periodic pension cost that would be reported in OCI is the remeasurements component. It consists of actuarial gains and losses on the pension obligation and net return on plan assets. Here, the actuarial loss was 460. In addition, the actual return on plan assets was 2,700, which was 30 lower than the return of 2,730 (= 39,000 × 0.07) incorporated in the net interest income/expense. Therefore, the total remeasurements are 490.

13. A is correct. In 2009, XYZ used a lower volatility assumption than it did in 2008. Lower expected volatility reduces the fair value of an option and thus the reported expense. Using the 2008 volatility estimate would have resulted in higher expense and thus lower net income.

14. C is correct. The assumed long-term rate of return on plan assets is not a component that is used in calculating the pension obligation, so there would be no change.

15. B is correct. A higher discount rate (5.38 percent instead of 4.85 percent) will reduce the present value of the pension obligation (liability). In most cases, a higher discount rate will

decrease the interest cost component of the net periodic cost because the decrease in the obligation will more than offset the increase in the discount rate (except if the pension obligation is of short duration). Therefore, periodic pension cost would have been lower and reported net income higher. Cash flow from operating activities should not be affected by the change.

16. B is correct. In 2009, the three relevant assumptions were lower than in 2008. Lower expected salary increases reduce the service cost component of the periodic pension cost. A lower discount rate will increase the defined benefit obligation and increase the interest cost component of the periodic pension cost (the increase in the obligation will, in most cases, more than offset the decrease in the discount rate). Reducing the expected return on plan assets typically increases the periodic pension cost.

17. A is correct. The company's inflation estimate rose from 2008 to 2009. However, it lowered its estimate of future salary increases. Normally, salary increases will be positively related to inflation.

18. B is correct. A higher volatility assumption increases the value of the stock option and thus the compensation expense, which, in turn, reduces net income. There is no associated liability for stock options.

19. C is correct. A higher dividend yield reduces the value of the option and thus option expense. The lower expense results in higher earnings. Higher risk-free rates and expected lives result in higher call option values.

CHAPTER 15

INTERCORPORATE
INVESTMENTS

SOLUTIONS

1. A is correct. Dividends from equity securities that are classified as available-for-sale are included in income when earned. Cinnamon would record its 19 percent share of the dividends paid by Cambridge; this is £3.8 million (£20 × 0.19). Though the value of Cinnamon's stake in Cambridge Processing rose by £2 million during the year, under IFRS any unrealized gains or losses for available-for-sale securities are reported in the equity section of the balance sheet as part of other comprehensive income until the securities are sold.

2. B is correct. If Cinnamon is deemed to have control over Cambridge, it would use the acquisition method to account for Cambridge and prepare consolidated financial statements. Proportionate consolidation is used for joint ventures; the equity method is used for some joint ventures and when there is significant influence but not control.

3. A is correct. If Cinnamon is deemed to have control over Cambridge, consolidated financial statements would be prepared and Cinnamon's shareholders' equity would increase and include the amount of the noncontrolling interest. If Cinnamon is deemed to have significant influence, the equity method would be used and there would be no change in the shareholders' equity of Cinnamon.

4. C is correct. If Cinnamon is deemed to have significant influence, it would report half of Cambridge's net income as a line item on its income statement, but no additional revenue is shown. Its profit margin is thus higher than if it consolidated Cambridge's results, which would impact revenue and income, or if it only reported 19 percent of Cambridge's dividends (no change in ownership).

5. C is correct. The full and partial goodwill method will have the same amount of debt; however, shareholders' equity will be higher under full goodwill (and the debt to equity ratio will be lower). Therefore, the debt to equity will be higher under partial goodwill. If control is assumed, Cinnamon cannot use the equity method.

6. A is correct. Cambridge has a lower operating margin (88/1,100 = 8.0%) than Cinnamon (142/1,575 = 9.0%). If Cambridge's results are consolidated with Cinnamon's, the consolidated operating margin will reflect that of the combined company, or 230/2,675 = 8.6%.

7. B is correct. Oxbow was classified as a held for trading security. Held for trading securities are reported at fair value, with unrealized gains and losses included in income. The income statement also includes dividends from equity securities that are classified as held for trading. The €3 million decline in the value of Zimt's stake would reduce income by that amount. Zimt would record its share of the dividends paid (0.1 × €20 million = €2 million). The net effect of Zimt's stake in Oxbow Limited would be to reduce Zimt's income before taxes by €1 million for 2009.

8. A is correct. When a company is deemed to have control of another entity, it records all of the other entity's assets on its own consolidated balance sheet.

9. B is correct. If Zimt is deemed to have significant influence, it would use the equity method to record its ownership. Under the equity method, Zimt's share of Oxbow's net income would be recorded as a single line item. Net income of Zimt = 75 + 0.5(68) = 109.

10. B is correct. Under the proportionate consolidation method, Zimt's balance sheet would show its own total liabilities of €1,421 – 735 = €686 plus half of Oxbow's liabilities of €1,283 – 706 = €577. €686 + (0.5 × 577) = €974.5.

11. C is correct. Under the assumption of control, Zimt would record its own sales plus 100 percent of Oxbow's. €1,700 + 1,350 = €3,050.

12. C is correct. Net income is not affected by the accounting method used to account for active investments in other companies. "One-line consolidation" and consolidation result in the same impact on net income; it is the disclosure that differs.

13. C is correct. Held for trading and available-for-sale securities are carried at market value, whereas held-to-maturity securities are carried at historical cost. €28,000 + 40,000 + 50,000 = €118,000.

14. C is correct. If Dumas had been classified as a held for trading security, its carrying value would have been the €55,000 fair value rather than the €50,000 historical cost.

15. B is correct. The coupon payment is recorded as interest income whether securities are held-to-maturity or available-for-sale. No adjustment is required for amortization since the bonds were bought at par.

16. B is correct. Unrealized gains and losses are included in income when securities are classified as held for trading securities. During 2009 there was an unrealized loss of €1,000.

17. B is correct. The difference between historical cost and par value must be amortized under the effective interest method. If the par value is less than the initial cost (stated interest rate is greater than the effective rate), the interest income would be lower than the interest received because of amortization of the premium.

18. B is correct. Under IFRS, SPEs must be consolidated if they are conducted for the benefit of the sponsoring entity. Further, under IFRS, SPEs cannot be classified as qualifying. Under US GAAP, qualifying SPEs (a classification which has been eliminated) do not have to be consolidated.

19. B is correct. Statewide Medical was accounted for under the pooling of interest method, which causes all of Statewide's assets and liabilities to be reported at historical book value. The excess of assets over liabilities generally is lower using the historical book value method than using the fair value method (this latter method must be used under currently required acquisition accounting). It would have no effect on revenue.

20. A is correct. Under the equity method, BetterCare would record its interest in the joint venture's net profit as a single line item, but would show no line-by-line contribution to revenues or expenses.

21. C is correct. Net income will be the same under the equity method and proportional consolidation. However, sales, cost of sales, and expenses are different because under the equity method the net effect of sales, cost of sales, and expenses is reflected in a single line.

22. B is correct. Under the proportionate consolidation method, Supreme Healthcare's consolidated financial statements will include its 50 percent share of the joint venture's total assets.

23. C is correct. The choice of equity method or proportionate consolidation does not affect reported shareholders' equity.

24. C is correct. Although Supreme Healthcare has no voting interest in the SPE, it is expected to absorb any losses that the SPE incurs. Therefore, Supreme Healthcare "in substance" controls the SPE and would consolidate it. On the consolidated balance sheet, the accounts receivable balance will be the same since the sale to the SPE will be reversed upon consolidation.

25. A is correct. The current ratio using the equity method of accounting is Current assets/ Current liabilities = £250/£110 = 2.27. Using consolidation (either full or partial goodwill), the current ratio = £390/£200 = 1.95. Therefore, the current ratio is highest using the equity method.

26. A is correct. Using the equity method, long-term debt to equity = £600/£1,430 = 0.42. Using the consolidation method, long-term debt to equity = long-term debt/equity = £1,000/£1,750 = 0.57. Equity includes the £320 noncontrolling interest under either consolidation. It does not matter if the full or partial goodwill method is used since there is no goodwill.

27. C is correct. The projected depreciation and amortization expense will include NinMount's reported depreciation and amortization (£102), Boswell's reported depreciation and amortization (£92), and amortization of Boswell's licenses (£10 million). The licenses have a fair value of £60 million. £320 purchase price indicates a fair value of £640 for the net assets of Boswell. The net book (fair) value of the recorded assets is £580. The previously unrecorded licenses have a fair value of £60 million. The licenses have a remaining life of six years; the amortization adjustment for 2008 will be £10 million. Therefore, projected depreciation and amortization = £102 + £92 + £10 = £204 million.

28. A is correct. Net income is the same using any of the methods but under the equity method, net sales are only £950; Boswell's sales are not included in the net sales figure. Therefore, net profit margin is highest using the equity method.

29. A is correct. Net income is the same using any of the choices. Beginning equity under the equity method is £1,430. Under either of the consolidations, beginning equity is £1,750 since it includes the £320 noncontrolling interest. Return on beginning equity is highest under the equity method.

30. A is correct. Using the equity method, Total asset turnover = Net sales/Beginning total assets = £950/£2,140 = 0.444. Total asset turnover on beginning assets using consolidation = £1,460/£2,950 = 0.495. Under consolidation, Assets = £2,140 – 320 + 1,070 + 60 = £2,950. Therefore, total asset turnover is lowest using the equity method.

CHAPTER 16

MULTINATIONAL OPERATIONS

SOLUTIONS

1. B is correct. IAS 21 requires that the financial statements of the foreign entity first be restated for local inflation using the procedures outlined in IAS 29, "Financial Reporting in Hyperinflationary Economies." Then, the inflation-restated foreign currency financial statements are translated into the parent's presentation currency using the current exchange rate. Under US GAAP, the temporal method would be used with no restatement.

2. B is correct. Ruiz expects the EUR to appreciate against the UAH and expects some inflation in the Ukraine. In an inflationary environment, FIFO will generate a higher gross profit than weighted-average cost. For either inventory choice, the current rate method will give higher gross profit to the parent company if the subsidiary's currency is depreciating. Thus, using FIFO and translating using the current rate method will generate a higher gross profit for the parent company, Eurexim SA, than any other combination of choices.

3. B is correct. If the parent's currency is chosen as the functional currency, the temporal method must be used. Under the temporal method, fixed assets are translated using the rate in effect at the time the assets were acquired.

4. C is correct. Monetary assets and liabilities such as accounts receivable are translated at current (end-of-period) rates regardless of whether the temporal or current rate method is used.

5. B is correct. When the foreign currency is chosen as the functional currency, the current rate method is used. All assets and liabilities are translated at the current (end-of-period) rate.

6. C is correct. When the foreign currency is chosen as the functional currency, the current rate method must be used and all gains or losses from translation are reported as a cumulative translation adjustment to shareholder equity. When the foreign currency decreases

in value (weakens), the current rate method results in a negative translation adjustment in stockholders' equity.

7. B is correct. When the parent company's currency is used as the functional currency, the temporal method must be used to translate the subsidiary's accounts. Under the temporal method, monetary assets and liabilities (e.g., debt) are translated at the current (year-end) rate, non-monetary assets and liabilities measured at historical cost (e.g., inventory) are translated at historical exchange rates, and non-monetary assets and liabilities measured at current value are translated at the exchange rate at the date when the current value was determined. Because beginning inventory was sold first and sales and purchases were evenly acquired, the average rate is most appropriate for translating inventory and C$77 million × 0.92 = $71 million. Long-term debt is translated at the year-end rate of 0.95. C$175 million × 0.95 = $166 million.

8. B is correct. Translating the 20X2 balance sheet using the temporal method, as is required in this instance, results in assets of US$369 million. The translated liabilities and common stock are equal to US$325 million, meaning that the value for 20X2 retained earnings is US$369 million − US$325 million = US$44 million.

Temporal Method (20X2)			
Account	C$	Rate	US$
Cash	135	0.95	128
Accounts receivable	98	0.95	93
Inventory	77	0.92	71
Fixed assets	100	0.86	86
Accumulated depreciation	(10)	0.86	(9)
Total assets	400		369
Accounts payable	77	0.95	73
Long-term debt	175	0.95	166
Common stock	100	0.86	86
Retained earnings	48	to balance	44
Total liabilities and shareholders' equity	400		369

9. C is correct. The Canadian dollar would be the appropriate reporting currency when substantially all operating, financing, and investing decisions are based on the local currency. The parent country's inflation rate is never relevant. Earnings manipulation is not justified, and at any rate changing the functional currency would take the gains off of the income statement.

10. C is correct. If the functional currency were changed from the parent currency (US dollar) to the local currency (Canadian dollar), the current rate method would replace the temporal method. The temporal method ignores unrealized gains and losses on non-monetary assets and liabilities, but the current rate method does not.

11. B is correct. If the Canadian dollar is chosen as the functional currency, the current rate method will be used and the current exchange rate will be the rate used to translate all assets and liabilities. Currently, only monetary assets and liabilities are translated at the

current rate. Sales are translated at the average rate during the year under either method. Fixed assets are translated using the historical rate under the temporal method but would switch to current rates under the current rate method. Therefore, there will most likely be an effect on sales/fixed assets. Because the cash ratio involves only monetary assets and liabilities, it is unaffected by the translation method. Receivables turnover pairs a monetary asset with sales and is thus also unaffected.

12. B is correct. If the functional currency were changed, then Consol-Can would use the current rate method and the balance sheet exposure would be equal to net assets (total assets − total liabilities). In this case, $400 − 77 − 175 = 148$.

13. B is correct. Julius is using the current rate method, which is most appropriate when it is operating with a high degree of autonomy.

14. A is correct. If the current rate method is being used (as it is for Julius), the local currency (euro) is the functional currency. When the temporal method is being used (as it is for Augustus), the parent company's currency (US dollar) is the functional currency.

15. C is correct. When the current rate method is being used, all currency gains and losses are recorded as a cumulative translation adjustment to shareholder equity.

16. C is correct. Under the current rate method, all assets are translated using the year-end 20X2 (current) rate of $1.61/€1.00. $€2,300 × 1.61 = \$3,703$.

17. A is correct. Under the current rate method, both sales and cost of goods sold would be translated at the 20X2 average exchange rate. The ratio would be the same as reported under the euro. $€2,300 − €1,400 = €900$, $€900/€2,300 = 39.1\%$. Or, $\$3,542 − \$2,156 = \$1,386$, $\$1,386/\$3,542 = 39.1\%$.

18. C is correct. Augustus is using the temporal method in conjunction with FIFO inventory accounting. If FIFO is used, ending inventory is assumed to be composed of the most recently acquired items, and thus inventory will be translated at relatively recent exchange rates. To the extent that the average weight used to translate sales differs from the historical rate used to translate inventories, the gross margin will be distorted when translated into US dollars.

19. C is correct. If the US dollar is the functional currency, the temporal method must be used. Revenues and receivables (monetary asset) would be the same under either accounting method. Inventory and fixed assets were purchased when the US dollar was stronger, so at historical rates (temporal method), translated they would be lower. Identical revenues/lower fixed assets would result in higher fixed-asset turnover.

20. A is correct. If the US dollar is the functional currency, the temporal method must be used, and the balance sheet exposure will be the net monetary assets of $125 + 230 − 185 − 200 = −30$, or a net monetary liability of SGD30 million. This net monetary liability would be eliminated if fixed assets (non-monetary) were sold to increase cash. Issuing debt, either short-term or long-term, would increase the net monetary liability.

21. A is correct. Because the US dollar has been consistently weakening against the Singapore dollar, cost of sales will be lower and gross profit higher when an earlier exchange rate is used to translate inventory, compared with using current exchange rates. If the Singapore dollar is the functional currency, current rates would be used. Therefore, the combination of the US dollar (temporal method) and FIFO will result in the highest gross profit margin.

22. A is correct. Under the current rate method, revenue is translated at the average rate for the year, SGD4,800 × 0.662 = USD3,178 million. Debt should be translated at the current rate, SGD200 × 0.671 = USD134 million. Under the current rate method, Acceletron would have a net asset balance sheet exposure. Because the Singapore dollar has been strengthening against the US dollar, the translation adjustment would be positive rather than negative.

23. B is correct. Under the temporal method, inventory and fixed assets would be translated using historical rates. Accounts receivable is a monetary asset and would be translated at year-end (current) rates. Fixed assets are found as (1,000 × 0.568) + (640 × 0.606) = USD 956 million.

24. B is correct. USD0.671/SGD is the current exchange rate. That rate would be used regardless of whether Acceletron uses the current rate or temporal method. USD0.654 was the weighted-average rate when inventory was acquired. That rate would be used if the company translated its statements under the temporal method but not the current rate method. USD0.588/SGD was the exchange rate in effect when long-term debt was issued. As a monetary liability, long-term debt is always translated using current exchange rates. Consequently, that rate is not applicable regardless of how Acceletron translates its financial statements.

CHAPTER 17

EVALUATING QUALITY OF FINANCIAL REPORTS

SOLUTIONS

1. B is correct. Stellar's financial statements are GAAP compliant (Conclusion 1) but cannot be relied upon to assess earnings quality. There is evidence of earnings management: understating and overstating earnings depending upon the results of the period (Conclusion 1), understated amortizable intangibles (Conclusion 2), and a high accruals component in the company's earnings (Conclusion 3).

2. C is correct. Martinez believes that Stellar most likely understated the value of amortizable intangibles when recording the acquisition of a rival company last year. Impairment charges have not been taken since the acquisition (Conclusion 2). Consequently, the company's earnings are likely to be overstated because amortization expense is understated. This understatement has not been offset by an impairment charge.

3. B is correct. Martinez concluded that the accruals component of Stellar's earnings was large relative to the cash component (Conclusion 3). Earnings with a larger component of accruals are typically less persistent and of lower quality. An important distinction is between accruals that arise from normal transactions in the period (called non-discretionary) and accruals that result from transactions or accounting choices outside the normal (called discretionary accruals). The discretionary accruals are possibly made with the intent to distort reported earnings. Outlier discretionary accruals are an indicator of possibly manipulated—and thus low quality earnings. Thus, Martinez is primarily focused on discretionary accruals, particularly outlier discretionary accruals (referred to as abnormal accruals).

4. B is correct. Because accounts receivable will be lower than reported in the past, Stellar's DSO [Accounts receivable/(Revenues/365)] will decrease. Stellar's accounts receivable turnover (365/days' sales outstanding) will increase with the lower DSO, giving the false impression of a faster turnover. The company's current ratio will decrease (current assets will decrease with no change in current liabilities).

CHAPTER 18

INTEGRATION OF FINANCIAL STATEMENT ANALYSIS TECHNIQUES

SOLUTIONS

1. A is correct. The capitalized value of Silk Road's leases, the amount by which assets would increase, is estimated as the present value of the operating lease expense (payments). The present value of 8 payments of 213 at 6.5 percent is 1,297.

2. B is correct. Adjusted EBIT = EBIT + Lease expense − Adjustment to depreciation = 318 + 213 − (1,297/8) = 369. Adjusted interest expense = Interest expense + Assumed interest expense on leases = 21 + (0.065 × 1,297) = 105.3. Adjusted interest coverage ratio = 369/105.3 = 3.50.

3. C is correct. The capitalized value of the leases is added to assets and liabilities but does not impact equity. On an adjusted basis, Silk Road's financial leverage ratio = (2,075 + 1,297)/1,156 = 2.92.

4. A is correct. Without the accounting change, Colorful Concepts has a financial leverage ratio = 3,844/2,562 = 1.50 and an interest coverage ratio = 865/35 = 24.71. These are both passing ratios. With the accounting change, the capitalized value of Colorful Concept's leases is 2,472. The financial leverage ratio = (3,844 + 2,472)/2,562 = 2.46 and the interest coverage ratio = [865 + 406 − (2,472/8)]/[35 + (2,472 × 0.065)] = 4.91. These are both failing ratios. The change in interest rate coverage is particularly dramatic.

5. A is correct. Silk Road has higher unadjusted and adjusted financial leverage ratios and lower unadjusted and adjusted interest coverage ratios than Colorful Concepts. Silk Road is riskier based on the financial leverage and interest coverage ratios, so it should have a lower bond rating.

6. B is correct. The investment in Exotic Imports is accounted for using the equity method and 20 percent of Exotic Import's net income is included in the net income of Colorful

Concepts. The net profit margin excluding the investment in Exotic Imports is (528 − 21)/7,049 = 7.2 percent. (If the investment in Exotic Imports is included, net profit margin is 7.5 percent.)

7. B is correct. The asset turnover ratio (sales/average total assets) without adjustment is 7,049/3,844 = 1.83. To compute the asset turnover ratio excluding investments in associates, the average investment in associates [(204 + 188)/2 = 196] is deducted from average total assets. The adjusted asset turnover ratio is 7,049/(3,844 − 196) = 1.93. The asset turnover ratio increased by 0.10.

8. C is correct. The calculation for interest coverage is EBIT/interest expense, neither of which is affected by the investment in associates.

9. C is correct. The ROE has been trending higher. ROE can be calculated by multiplying (net profit margin) × (asset turnover) × (financial leverage). Net profit margin is net income/sales. In 2007 the net profit margin was 2,576/55,781 = 4.6% and the ROE = 4.6% × 0.68 × 3.43 = 10.8%. Using the same method, ROE was 12.9 percent in 2008 and 13.6 percent in 2009.

10. A is correct. The DuPont analysis shows that profit margins and asset turnover have both increased over the last three years, but leverage has declined. The reduction in leverage offsets a portion of the improvement in profitability and turnover. Thus, ROE would have been higher if leverage had not decreased.

11. B is correct. The Power and Industrial segment has the lowest EBIT margins but uses about 31 percent of the capital employed. Further, Power and Industrial's proportion of the capital expenditures has increased from 32 percent to 36 percent over the three years. Its capital intensity only looked to get worse, as the segment's percentage of total capital expenditures was higher than its percentage of total capital in each of the three years. If Abay is considering divesting segments that do not earn sufficient returns on capital employed, this segment is most suitable.

12. A is correct. The cash-flow-based accruals ratio = [NI − (CFO + CFI)]/(Average NOA) = [4,038 − (9,822 − 10,068)]/43,192 = 9.9%.

13. A is correct. The cash-flow-based accruals ratio falls from 11.0 percent in 2007 to 5.9 percent in 2008, and then rises to 9.9 percent in 2009. However, the change over the three-year period is a net modest decline, indicating a slight improvement in earnings quality.

14. B is correct. Net cash flow provided by (used in) operating activity has to be adjusted for interest and taxes, as necessary, in order to be comparable to operating income (EBIT). Bickchip, reporting under IFRS, chose to classify interest expense as a financing cash flow so the only necessary adjustment is for taxes. The operating cash flow before interest and taxes = 9,822 + 1,930 = 11,752. Dividing this by EBIT of 6,270 yields 1.9.

15. A is correct. Operating cash flow before interest and taxes to operating income rises steadily (not erratically) from 1.2 to 1.3 to 1.9. The ratios over 1.0 and the trend indicate that earnings are supported by cash flow.

16. A is correct. The leverage ratio is measured as total assets/total equity. As reported, this was $3,610,600/$976,500 = 3.70. Had the securitized receivables been held on the balance sheet, assets would have been $267,500 higher, or $3,878,100, and equity would have

been unchanged. The ratio would then have been 3.97. The ratio of 3.70 as reported is 6.8 percent less than 3.97: $1 - 3.7/3.97 = 0.068$.

17. B is correct. If the receivables had been held on the balance sheet, both assets and liabilities would have been $267,500 higher: $2,901,600/$3,878,100 = 74.8\%$.

18. A is correct. PDQ owns 20 percent of Astana ($0.2 \times 298,350 = \$59,670$). Translated at the current exchange rate of $1.62 per euro that is €36,833. $36,833/563,355 = 0.0654$ or 6.5%.

19. A is correct. PDQ's solo market capitalization is $563,355 - 36,833 = 526,522$. To calculate its solo net income, because Astana is accounted for using the equity method, 20 percent of Astana's net income of $9,945 is translated at the average exchange rate of $1.55/€ and deducted from PDQ's net income to produce €26,884 in adjusted net income for PDQ. $P/E = 526,522/26,884 = 19.6$.

20. B is correct. Adjusted financial statements are created during the data processing phase of the financial analysis process.

21. A is correct. Estimates of Astana's impact on PDQ's financial statements are crude due to the potential differences in accounting standards used by the two firms. Based on the currencies each reports in, Astana is likely using US GAAP and PDQ is likely using IFRS. Pricing (market capitalization) should reflect the other potential differences.

ABOUT THE
CFA PROGRAM

The Chartered Financial Analyst® designation (CFA®) is a globally recognized standard of excellence for measuring the competence and integrity of investment professionals. To earn the CFA charter, candidates must successfully pass through the CFA Program, a global graduate-level self-study program that combines a broad curriculum with professional conduct requirements as preparation for a wide range of investment specialties.

Anchored by a practice-based curriculum, the CFA Program is focused on the knowledge identified by professionals as essential to the investment decision-making process. This body of knowledge maintains current relevance through a regular, extensive survey of practicing CFA charterholders across the globe. The curriculum covers 10 general topic areas, ranging from equity and fixed-income analysis to portfolio management to corporate finance, all with a heavy emphasis on the application of ethics in professional practice. Known for its rigor and breadth, the CFA Program curriculum highlights principles common to every market so that professionals who earn the CFA designation have a thoroughly global investment perspective and a profound understanding of the global marketplace.

www.cfainstitute.org